Learn Swift for Augmented Reality (AR) Development

Build AR Applications for iOS with Swift and ARKit

Greyson Chesterfield

COPYRIGHT

DISCLAIMER

The information provided in this book is for general informational purposes only. All content in this book reflects the author's views and is based on their research, knowledge, and experiences. The author and publisher make no representations or warranties of any kind concerning the completeness, accuracy, reliability, suitability, or availability of the information contained herein.

This book is not intended to be a substitute for professional advice, diagnosis, or treatment. Readers should seek professional advice for any specific concerns or conditions. The author and publisher disclaim any liability or responsibility for any direct, indirect, incidental, or consequential loss or damage arising from the use of the information contained in this book.

Contents

Chapter 1: Introduction to Augmented Reality (AR) 6

1.1 History and Evolution of AR in Everyday Tech 6

1.2 Popular AR Applications and Their Impact 8

1.3 Overview of AR Potential on iOS Devices 10

Chapter 2: Why Swift and ARKit? 13

2.1 Benefits of Swift for AR Development 13

2.2 Introduction to ARKit: Capabilities and Compatibility 15

2.3 Setting Up for Success: Key Tools and Resources 18

Chapter 3: Preparing Your Development Environment 22

3.1 Installing and Configuring Xcode for AR Projects 22

3.2 Overview of ARKit Libraries and Resources.....................24

3.3 First Project Setup: Creating a "Hello AR" Demo App 27

Chapter 4: Swift Fundamentals for AR Development 31

4.1 Core Swift Concepts Needed for AR: Variables, Functions, and Classes 31

4.2 How AR Differs in Swift: Practical Examples 35

4.3 Structuring Code for Efficiency and Readability in AR Applications 38

Chapter 5: Understanding 3D Space and Coordinate Systems ..43

5.1 Basics of 3D Space: Coordinate Systems and Object Placement 43

5.2 Orientation, Positioning, and Scaling in ARKit...................45

5.3 Practical Exercise: Placing a Virtual Object in Real-World Space 48

Chapter 6: Building Interactive AR Scenes with SceneKit........54

6.1 Basics of SceneKit for 3D Object Rendering.....................54

6.2 Adding Lights, Textures, and Colors to 3D Objects.........................57

6.3 Example Project: Designing a Basic AR Scene 60

Chapter 7: User Interaction in AR Applications 66

7.1 Understanding and Implementing Touch and Gesture Recognizers 66

7.2 Designing User Interfaces (UI) for Immersive AR Experiences......70

7.3 Real-World Example: Building an Interactive Product Viewer 73

Chapter 8: Working with Real-World Anchors.........................79

8.1 Introduction to AR Anchors and Their Purpose 79

8.2 Types of Anchors: Plane, Image, and Object Anchors.....................81

8.3 Practical Application: Anchoring Virtual Objects to Real-World Surfaces...86

Chapter 9: Animating AR Objects 92

9.1 Basics of Animation in AR Using Swift and SceneKit.....................92

9.2 Key Techniques: Moving, Rotating, and Scaling Objects...............95

9.3 Example Project: Animating Objects to Follow User Interactions.98

Chapter 10: Using Physics in AR Environments 105

10.1 Overview of Physics in AR: Gravity, Collision, and Dynamics...105

10.2 Applying Physics to 3D Objects for Realism.................................108

10.3 Practical Example: Creating a Simple Physics-Based AR Simulation...111

Chapter 11: Exploring Advanced Object Recognition............118

11.1 Implementing Image and Object Recognition with ARKit.........118

11.2 Using Real-World Objects as Interactive Triggers.......................122

11.3 Real-World Application: Designing an AR App that Recognizes and Reacts to Objects 125

Chapter 12: Lighting and Shadows for Realism......................132

12.1 Understanding AR Lighting: Ambient and Directional Light 132

12.2 Light Estimation for Dynamic Environments...............................135

12.3 Enhancing Realism with Shadows: Practical Application 138

Chapter 13: Building an AR Game (Part 1) 145

13.1 Planning an AR Game: Concept, Design, and User Experience .145

13.2 Setting Up the Game's Environment and Elements 148

13.3 Example Project: Building a Virtual Shooting Game 152

Chapter 14: Building an AR Game (Part 2) 158

14.1 Adding Interactivity: User Controls, Scoring, and Feedback 158

14.2 Integrating Physics for Gameplay Mechanics...............................162

14.3 Testing and Refining for a Smooth Player Experience 166

Chapter 15: ARKit and SwiftUI for Enhanced User Experiences
....171

15.1 Using SwiftUI for AR User Interfaces 171

15.2 Creating AR Interfaces That Are Responsive and User-Friendly
....175

15.3 Example Project: Building an AR Gallery with SwiftUI 179

Chapter 16: Optimizing AR Performance for iOS 188

16.1 Techniques for Efficient AR App Performance...........................188

16.2 Managing Memory, Frame Rates, and Battery Life in AR Apps192

**16.3 Practical Tips: Optimization Strategies for Smooth AR
Experiences**..194

Chapter 17: Publishing and Marketing Your AR App 201

17.1 Preparing Your AR App for the App Store: Guidelines and Tips
....201

17.2 App Store Optimization (ASO) Strategies for AR Apps.............204

17.3 Promoting Your AR App: Marketing Channels and Best Practices
....206

Chapter 18: Future of AR and Continuous Learning 212

18.1 Emerging Trends in AR and Potential New Features in ARKit .212

18.2 Expanding Your AR Knowledge: Resources and Communities .215

18.3 Long-Term Outlook: How AR is Shaping Future User Experiences
....218

Chapter 1: Introduction to Augmented Reality (AR)

1.1 History and Evolution of AR in Everyday Tech

1.1.1 Origins and Early Concepts

- **Conceptual Beginnings**: The idea of augmenting our view of the real world dates back decades. Early AR concepts were explored as far back as the 1960s when computer scientist Ivan Sutherland designed the first head-mounted display (HMD) device, called the "Sword of Damocles." Although it was rudimentary, Sutherland's device laid the foundation for augmented reality.

- **Early Examples and Milestones**: In the 1990s, Boeing researchers developed a wearable display to aid in airplane construction, marking one of the first practical uses of AR. Around the same time, software advances enabled basic AR applications, like overlaying information on video feeds.

1.1.2 Rise of AR in Gaming and Commercial Use

- **Gaming Influence**: AR gaming gained mainstream attention in the early 2000s with the Nintendo Game Boy and early handheld consoles. By the 2010s, with the release of mobile games like *Pokémon Go*, AR had captured global attention, demonstrating how people could interact with virtual objects overlaid on the real world.

- **Commercial Adoption**: AR evolved further as companies like IKEA, Sephora, and others developed applications to enhance the shopping experience. These apps allowed users to "try before they buy" with virtual furniture or cosmetics in real-time, transforming the way customers interacted with products.

1.1.3 Recent Advances and Current State

- **Smartphones and Wearables**: The introduction of ARKit by Apple in 2017 marked a significant leap, allowing developers to harness the power of iOS devices to create sophisticated AR experiences. This era saw widespread use of AR across devices like smartphones and wearables, making AR more accessible than ever.

- **Evolving AR Technologies**: Today, AR incorporates AI, machine learning, and advanced 3D modeling, allowing for realistic, dynamic, and responsive applications across multiple industries, from healthcare to education.

1.2 Popular AR Applications and Their Impact

1.2.1 Gaming and Entertainment

- **Example: Pokémon Go**: The groundbreaking mobile game introduced AR to millions, allowing users to catch virtual creatures superimposed on real-world locations. *Pokémon Go* not only popularized AR but also encouraged exploration and social interaction.

- **Social Media Filters**: Apps like Snapchat and Instagram utilize AR to enhance user experience through face filters and effects, making AR a key feature in social engagement and personal expression.

1.2.2 Retail and Shopping

- **In-Store Experiences**: Companies like IKEA use AR to allow users to visualize furniture in their home environment, helping customers make informed purchase decisions. Similarly, beauty brands like Sephora and L'Oréal offer AR-powered apps for virtual makeovers, significantly influencing customer engagement and satisfaction.

- **Impact on Consumer Behavior**: AR in retail is changing how people shop, allowing them to test products virtually, which in turn reduces return rates and enhances customer satisfaction.

1.2.3 Healthcare and Education

- **Training and Simulation**: In healthcare, AR applications assist with medical training by overlaying digital information onto physical bodies or medical equipment, allowing practitioners to simulate procedures. This hands-on approach improves learning outcomes and reduces risks associated with real-life training.

- **Educational Tools**: AR has proven effective in education, especially for subjects like anatomy, astronomy, and history. AR applications make learning interactive and immersive, which is particularly engaging for students of all ages.

1.2.4 Navigation and Mapping

- **Google Maps and Apple Maps AR**: Both Google and Apple have incorporated AR features into their mapping services, providing real-time guidance by overlaying directional arrows on a live video feed of the user's surroundings. This not only enhances accuracy but also simplifies navigation for users.

- **Impact on Tourism and Travel**: AR-enabled mapping apps assist travelers in navigating unfamiliar locations with ease, transforming how people explore new places by offering real-time information about landmarks and businesses nearby.

1.3 Overview of AR Potential on iOS Devices

1.3.1 Apple's Commitment to AR Development

- **ARKit and iOS Devices**: Since Apple introduced ARKit, the company has consistently updated the framework, giving developers new tools to create sophisticated AR applications. iOS devices are equipped with cameras, LiDAR scanners, and powerful processors, making them ideal platforms for AR.

- **Integration with Apple Ecosystem**: Apple has integrated AR across its ecosystem, from iPhones and iPads to Macs, enabling seamless transitions between devices and fostering cross-device AR experiences. Features like *Measure*, an iOS app that allows users to measure physical spaces, are examples of Apple's push to incorporate AR into daily utilities.

1.3.2 AR Applications on iOS

- **Education and Learning**: Apps like Froggipedia and Complete Anatomy leverage ARKit to offer immersive educational experiences on iOS, demonstrating how AR can transform traditional learning into a hands-on, interactive experience.

- **Shopping and Lifestyle**: Retail applications like IKEA Place and Home Depot leverage ARKit to help users visualize products in real-world environments. These applications, coupled with Apple's high-resolution displays and processing power, set iOS devices apart in delivering smooth, high-quality AR interactions.

1.3.3 The Future of AR on iOS

- **Continued Hardware Advancements**: Apple's commitment to hardware advancements, particularly with its custom processors and LiDAR technology, means that iOS devices are likely to support even more complex and realistic AR applications in the future.

- **Integration with Emerging Technologies**: As AR continues to evolve, Apple is likely to integrate it further with technologies like artificial intelligence, machine learning, and wearable tech. This could lead to enhanced applications in areas like healthcare, retail, and education, placing AR at the forefront of user interaction on iOS.

Chapter 2: Why Swift and ARKit?

2.1 Benefits of Swift for AR Development

2.1.1 The Design of Swift for Modern App Development

- **Developer-Friendly Syntax**: Swift is known for its clean, easy-to-read syntax, making it a beginner-friendly language for developers diving into iOS and AR development. This simplicity enables developers to build sophisticated applications with less code and fewer errors, speeding up the development process.

- **Strong Type Safety and Error Handling**: Swift's type safety feature prevents common programming errors, such as null pointer exceptions, ensuring a more stable development environment. Swift's error-handling capabilities enable developers to anticipate potential issues, which is crucial in AR applications where interaction with real-world objects can introduce unexpected variables.

2.1.2 Swift's High Performance

- **Optimized for Performance and Speed**: Swift is built with performance in mind, making it one of the fastest languages for developing mobile applications. Its speed is comparable to that of C++, which is beneficial for AR applications that rely heavily on real-time data processing and rendering.

- **Memory Management with ARC**: Automatic Reference Counting (ARC) in Swift helps developers manage memory usage efficiently. In AR applications, where objects may frequently be added or removed from the view, effective memory management is essential for maintaining smooth, responsive experiences.

2.1.3 Compatibility with Apple's Ecosystem

- **Integration with iOS, macOS, and watchOS**: Swift is the primary language for Apple's ecosystem, making it the ideal choice for AR applications that may extend beyond iPhones and iPads to Apple Watches and Macs. This versatility allows developers to create multi-platform AR experiences that interact seamlessly within Apple's ecosystem.

- **Community and Support**: Swift has a large, active developer community, providing resources, libraries, and forums for troubleshooting and collaboration. Apple's support for Swift continues to grow, with frequent updates and integrations with other

Apple tools, keeping the language at the forefront of iOS development.

2.2 Introduction to ARKit: Capabilities and Compatibility

2.2.1 ARKit's Core Capabilities

- **Tracking and Anchoring**: ARKit provides precise tracking capabilities, enabling devices to understand and interpret the environment in real time. It supports both *world tracking*, which lets the device track its position relative to the environment, and *image tracking*, allowing ARKit to detect and respond to images placed in the real world.

- **Plane Detection**: ARKit automatically detects flat surfaces, such as floors or tables, which are common areas where virtual objects are anchored. This detection is critical for accurate placement of objects, making it feel like they truly belong in the real environment.

- **Light Estimation**: ARKit includes advanced light estimation to make virtual objects match the lighting conditions of the environment. This feature enhances the realism of AR scenes, helping virtual objects blend seamlessly with the real world.

2.2.2 Extended Capabilities in ARKit Updates

- **Face Tracking**: In recent updates, ARKit has included advanced face tracking, allowing apps to map facial features in real-time. This has opened up opportunities for AR experiences in entertainment, social media, and customization, such as apps that let users try on virtual cosmetics or accessories.

- **LiDAR Support**: With the introduction of LiDAR sensors in newer iPhone and iPad models, ARKit can now capture depth information with even greater precision. LiDAR enables the creation of complex and realistic AR experiences by offering improved spatial understanding, especially in low-light conditions.

- **People Occlusion and Object Occlusion**: This feature allows virtual objects to interact naturally with real people or objects by visually "hiding" behind them when necessary, creating a more immersive AR experience. For example, a virtual object can appear behind a real chair in a room, making the experience more realistic.

2.2.3 Compatibility Across Apple Devices

- **Supported Devices and Performance Optimization**: ARKit is compatible with a wide range of iOS devices, starting with iPhones and iPads that have an A9 processor or newer. However, newer devices equipped with LiDAR sensors and advanced processors offer superior performance, enabling more complex AR applications.

- **Cross-Platform Integration**: ARKit integrates seamlessly with other Apple frameworks, such as SceneKit for 3D graphics, UIKit for user interfaces, and CoreML for machine learning. This compatibility enables developers to create multifaceted applications that leverage multiple technologies within a single, cohesive AR experience.

2.3 Setting Up for Success: Key Tools and Resources

2.3.1 Essential Tools for AR Development

- **Xcode**: Xcode is Apple's integrated development environment (IDE) and is the central hub for AR development on iOS. It provides a user-friendly interface for coding, debugging, and testing applications, making it essential for Swift and ARKit projects. Xcode includes a powerful AR simulator that allows developers to test AR applications directly on their Mac without needing a physical device, which is especially useful for initial testing and prototyping.

- **Reality Composer**: Reality Composer is an intuitive tool included in Xcode, specifically designed for creating and prototyping AR content. It enables developers to design, place, and animate virtual objects within a real-world setting, providing a fast way to visualize and test ideas. The drag-and-drop interface makes it accessible, even for developers without extensive 3D modeling experience.

- **SceneKit**: While not exclusive to ARKit, SceneKit is a 3D graphics framework that integrates well with ARKit for rendering 3D objects. SceneKit's capabilities include animations, particle effects, and lighting, making it invaluable for creating interactive and realistic AR experiences.

2.3.2 Supporting Libraries and Resources

- **ARKit Samples and Documentation**: Apple provides extensive ARKit documentation and sample projects that demonstrate ARKit's capabilities. These resources are invaluable for understanding ARKit's functions, troubleshooting issues, and learning best practices in AR development.

- **Swift Playgrounds**: Swift Playgrounds is an interactive app for learning Swift, offering hands-on tutorials and exercises. For developers new to Swift or AR, Swift Playgrounds provides a structured way to build foundational skills before moving on to more complex AR applications.

- **ARKit Community and Forums**:
  Communities like Stack Overflow, Apple
  Developer Forums, and dedicated ARKit
  groups are excellent resources for
  troubleshooting, discussing ideas, and staying
  updated on the latest advancements in AR
  technology. Engaging with these communities
  can help developers gain insights, troubleshoot
  issues faster, and learn from the experiences of
  others.

2.3.3 Best Practices for Success in AR Development

- **Starting Small and Iterating**: For developers
  new to AR, starting with a small project, like a
  basic object-placement app, is ideal. This
  approach allows them to familiarize themselves
  with ARKit's tools and gradually build more
  complex features.

- **Testing on Real Devices**: While Xcode's
  simulator is useful, testing on actual iOS
  devices is essential for evaluating performance
  in real-world environments. Different lighting
  conditions, surfaces, and surroundings can
  impact an AR app's behavior, so physical
  testing provides insights that simulators may
  not reveal.

- **Optimizing for Performance**: AR applications
  are data-intensive, so optimizing for
  performance is crucial. This includes managing
  memory effectively, minimizing the number of

3D assets, and using lower polygon counts when possible to ensure a smooth experience. Performance profiling tools in Xcode can assist in identifying potential bottlenecks.

Chapter 3: Preparing Your Development Environment

3.1 Installing and Configuring Xcode for AR Projects

3.1.1 Introduction to Xcode for AR Development

- **What is Xcode?**: Xcode is Apple's Integrated Development Environment (IDE) designed for iOS, macOS, watchOS, and tvOS app development. For AR projects, Xcode provides a streamlined interface for building, testing, and deploying apps using ARKit.

- **Why Xcode is Essential for AR Development**: Xcode includes specialized tools, like the AR Simulator and Reality Composer, which make it ideal for developing, debugging, and refining AR applications. These tools allow developers to see and test AR functionality before deploying to a physical device.

3.1.2 Installing Xcode

- **System Requirements**: Xcode requires macOS, so developers need a Mac or Mac-powered cloud environment. The minimum macOS version may vary with Xcode updates, so it's essential to check compatibility on the Apple Developer website.

- **Downloading Xcode**: Xcode can be downloaded from the Mac App Store. A reliable internet connection is recommended as Xcode's installation file is typically large, exceeding several gigabytes.

- **Initial Configuration**: After installation, launch Xcode and ensure all necessary components are updated. Xcode frequently prompts users to install additional tools required for Swift and ARKit development. Updating regularly ensures compatibility with the latest features and APIs.

3.1.3 Setting Up Your First Xcode Project

- **Creating a New Project**: Open Xcode, select "Create a new Xcode project," and choose the "Augmented Reality App" template under iOS. This template pre-configures the project with ARKit libraries, saving setup time.

- **Choosing a Language and Framework**: Set Swift as the programming language and SceneKit as the primary graphics framework. SceneKit is often preferred for ARKit because it integrates well with 3D rendering, which is essential for AR applications.

- **Project Configuration**: Name your project, specify the organization identifier, and choose the iOS version that matches your target device compatibility. Apple recommends setting the deployment target to the most recent stable iOS version for optimal performance.

3.2 Overview of ARKit Libraries and Resources

3.2.1 Understanding ARKit's Core Libraries

- **ARKit Framework**: ARKit is Apple's proprietary augmented reality framework that allows developers to create immersive experiences by blending virtual content with the physical world. The ARKit framework includes functionalities such as world tracking, plane detection, and light estimation, which are essential for realistic AR experiences.

- **SceneKit**: SceneKit is a 3D graphics framework compatible with ARKit, enabling developers to render 3D objects in AR scenes. SceneKit simplifies working with 3D content, including textures, lighting, and animations, which are crucial for dynamic AR applications.

- **RealityKit**: RealityKit is an alternative to SceneKit, specifically designed for AR. It offers more advanced features like dynamic lighting, environment textures, and physics-based rendering, making it suitable for high-quality AR experiences. While RealityKit is powerful, it may require more advanced understanding, making it ideal for more complex AR applications.

3.2.2 ARKit Libraries and Tools in Xcode

- **Reality Composer**: Reality Composer is a built-in tool within Xcode that simplifies the creation and arrangement of AR scenes. It allows developers to drag and drop objects, set animations, and experiment with interactions without writing code, making it a valuable resource for prototyping AR content.

- **AR Quick Look**: AR Quick Look allows users to view and interact with 3D models directly from an app or Safari. It supports USDZ files, Apple's proprietary 3D file format, which allows for seamless integration of 3D content in AR apps and enhances user experience with pre-configured, interactive models.

- **AR Simulator**: Xcode's AR Simulator allows developers to preview AR applications without a physical device. It simulates ARKit functionalities and provides a virtual environment for testing app performance, which is especially helpful in the early stages of development.

3.2.3 Essential Resources for AR Development with ARKit

- **Apple's Developer Documentation**: Apple offers comprehensive ARKit documentation, including guides, API references, and sample projects. These resources help developers understand ARKit's features and best practices for creating immersive AR applications.

- **Online Courses and Tutorials**: Platforms like Udacity, Coursera, and Apple's own Swift Playgrounds provide structured courses on AR development using Swift and ARKit. These tutorials are invaluable for beginners and offer step-by-step guidance in AR programming.

- **Community and Forums**: Joining ARKit developer communities on platforms like Stack Overflow, GitHub, and the Apple Developer Forums can be beneficial for troubleshooting and networking with other AR developers. Engaging in these communities can provide valuable insights and inspiration for AR projects.

3.3 First Project Setup: Creating a "Hello AR" Demo App

3.3.1 Creating the "Hello AR" Project

- **Setting Up the AR Scene**: After creating a new AR project in Xcode, developers are presented with a default AR scene that includes a placeholder 3D object. In this case, remove the placeholder and replace it with a custom 3D object, such as a simple box or sphere, to personalize the "Hello AR" app.

- **Configuring the AR Session**: AR sessions are the backbone of any ARKit application, as they handle camera input, object tracking, and environment processing. Initialize an ARSession in the project, configuring it for basic *world tracking*, which is necessary to detect horizontal planes and maintain object positioning.

- **Adding an Object to the Scene**: Using SceneKit or RealityKit, insert a basic 3D object into the AR view. For this demo, a simple cube can be added to the scene by initializing a SCNBox in SceneKit, or using Reality Composer to drag and drop a pre-built cube into the scene.

3.3.2 Coding the Core Features of "Hello AR"

- **Setting Up the ARView**: The ARView is the main interface through which users interact with the AR scene. Use ARSCNView (for SceneKit) or ARView (for RealityKit) to display and manage 3D content. Customize the view's properties, such as setting automatic lighting adjustments, to enhance realism.

- **Adding Gesture Controls**: Basic touch gestures make AR interactions intuitive. Set up gesture recognizers, such as tap gestures, to allow users to place the cube on a detected plane. This interactivity makes the app more engaging and demonstrates how users can interact with AR objects in real-world environments.

- **Testing the Project**: With the basic components in place, run the project in Xcode to test on an AR-capable iOS device. Observing the app on a physical device lets developers ensure that objects align correctly with real-world surfaces and respond to user interactions as expected.

3.3.3 Enhancing the Demo with Simple Animations

- **Adding Rotation or Scale Animations**: To add life to the "Hello AR" demo, create simple animations, like rotating or scaling the cube. Using SCNAction, developers can add animations with minimal code, making the cube spin or grow and shrink when tapped.

- **Experimenting with Light and Shadow**: ARKit's light estimation allows virtual objects to reflect real-world lighting conditions, creating a more immersive experience. Adjust the lighting properties of the scene or add a virtual light source to create shadows, which helps integrate the cube more naturally with the surroundings.

- **Expanding Interactivity**: Experiment with additional gestures, such as swipes or pinches, to further enhance the demo. For example, a swipe gesture could change the color of the cube, while a pinch could scale it up or down.

Chapter 4: Swift Fundamentals for AR Development

4.1 Core Swift Concepts Needed for AR: Variables, Functions, and Classes

4.1.1 Variables and Constants

- **Using Variables (var)**: In Swift, variables are declared using var and are mutable, meaning they can be modified after being assigned a value. Variables are particularly useful in AR applications where certain elements (like object positions or color) might change dynamically based on user interactions.

  - *Example*: var objectPosition = SCNVector3(x: 0, y: 0, z: 0) to define an initial position for a 3D object that might later change based on user input.

- **Constants (let)**: Constants are declared with let and are immutable, meaning they cannot be modified once assigned. Constants are used for fixed values that don't change throughout the app, helping prevent accidental overwrites and improving code reliability.

- *Example*: let initialObjectSize = SCNVector3(x: 0.5, y: 0.5, z: 0.5) to set an object's initial size if it should remain fixed.

4.1.2 Functions

- **Function Definition and Usage**: Functions in Swift are blocks of reusable code that perform specific tasks, improving code organization and reusability. Functions play a significant role in AR apps, where tasks like setting up objects, handling user input, or performing calculations are common.

  - *Syntax*: func functionName(parameters) -> ReturnType { /* code */ }

  - *Example*: A function to set up a 3D object in AR:

swift

```swift
func createCube(size: CGFloat) -> SCNBox {

    return SCNBox(width: size, height: size, length: size, chamferRadius: 0)

}
```

- **Parameters and Return Types**: Functions in Swift can take parameters and return values. In AR development, parameterized functions can be used to pass dynamic values like object size, color, or position, making functions flexible and reusable.

- o *Example*: func moveObject(to position: SCNVector3) -> Void to update the position of an object based on user actions.

4.1.3 Classes and Structs

- **Classes for Object-Oriented Programming**: Swift's class keyword defines classes, which are reference types and allow object-oriented programming (OOP) principles like inheritance and polymorphism. In AR development, classes can represent 3D objects or user interactions, enabling modular, structured code.

  - o *Example*: Creating a VirtualObject class to represent 3D objects in an AR scene:

swift

```swift
class VirtualObject {
    var position: SCNVector3
    var color: UIColor
    init(position: SCNVector3, color: UIColor) {
        self.position = position
        self.color = color
```

```
    }

}
```

- **Structs as Lightweight Data Containers**:
  struct is a value type that is often used for data
  models that don't require inheritance. Structs
  are ideal for representing simple, immutable
  data in AR apps, such as configurations or
  settings.

  - *Example*: struct ObjectProperties { var
    color: UIColor; var size: CGFloat } to
    define a fixed set of properties for AR
    objects.

4.2 How AR Differs in Swift: Practical Examples

4.2.1 Using SceneKit with Swift for 3D Objects

- **Creating and Positioning 3D Objects**:
  SceneKit makes it straightforward to create and
  manipulate 3D objects in Swift. Swift code
  allows precise control over attributes like
  position, size, and color, essential for
  customizing AR interactions.

  - *Example*: Adding a cube to an AR scene:

swift

```swift
let cube = SCNBox(width: 0.1, height: 0.1, length: 0.1,
chamferRadius: 0)

let cubeNode = SCNNode(geometry: cube)

cubeNode.position = SCNVector3(0, 0, -0.5) // Place it
half a meter in front of the user

scene.rootNode.addChildNode(cubeNode)
```

- **Handling Real-World Interactions**: Swift allows developers to respond to user actions by adjusting object properties. For instance, when a user taps the screen, an object's color can change, or it can be moved to a new location in real space.

4.2.2 Working with AR Anchors

- **Anchor-Based Object Placement**: In AR, anchors are used to fix virtual objects to real-world surfaces. ARKit's ARAnchor class allows Swift code to place objects with stability and reliability in the AR environment.

    - *Example*: Placing an object on a detected horizontal plane:

swift

```swift
func placeObject(at anchor: ARAnchor) {
```

```swift
let cube = createCube(size: 0.1)

let cubeNode = SCNNode(geometry: cube)

cubeNode.position =
SCNVector3(anchor.transform.columns.3.x,

            anchor.transform.columns.3.y,

            anchor.transform.columns.3.z)

scene.rootNode.addChildNode(cubeNode)
}
```

- **Plane Detection and Updating**: ARKit can detect horizontal and vertical planes, which are represented as anchors. When Swift code detects a plane, objects can be placed or moved dynamically based on the plane's position.

4.2.3 Light Estimation and Scene Adaptation

- **Adjusting to Real-World Lighting**: ARKit offers real-time light estimation to adapt virtual objects' lighting to match the environment. Swift enables seamless adjustments to object lighting, making objects appear more realistic in different lighting conditions.

  - *Example*: Applying light estimation in Swift:

swift

```swift
func updateLighting(with frame: ARFrame) {

    if let lightEstimate = frame.lightEstimate {

      let intensity = lightEstimate.ambientIntensity /
1000

      sceneView.scene.lightingEnvironment.intensity =
intensity

    }

}
```

4.3 Structuring Code for Efficiency and Readability in AR Applications

4.3.1 Using Extensions for Code Organization

- **Extensions to Modularize Code**: Swift's extensions enable developers to split large classes into smaller, focused sections, which is essential for managing AR projects. Using extensions to organize code into distinct functionalities (e.g., rendering, gesture handling, UI updates) improves readability and maintainability.

    - *Example*: Extension for gesture handling in an AR app:

swift

```swift
extension ViewController {

    @objc func handleTapGesture(_ sender:
UITapGestureRecognizer) {

        // Code to handle tap gesture

    }

}
```

4.3.2 Leveraging Protocols for Code Reusability

- **Protocols for Standardized Behavior**:
  Protocols define a set of required functions or
  properties, enabling standardized behaviors
  across different classes. In AR, protocols can be
  used to define shared actions, such as
  interaction behaviors or object properties, which
  can be reused across various objects.

  - *Example*: A protocol for interactive AR
    objects:

swift

```swift
protocol InteractiveObject {

    func onTap()

    func onDrag()

}
class Cube: InteractiveObject {
```

```swift
func onTap() { /* Define tap behavior */ }

func onDrag() { /* Define drag behavior */ }

}
```

4.3.3 Handling Asynchronous Tasks with Closures and Grand Central Dispatch (GCD)

- **Using Closures for Event-Driven Tasks**: Closures allow developers to handle asynchronous tasks, such as network requests or sensor data processing, directly in the flow of their code. In AR, closures are often used to handle user input or real-time data from ARKit.

    - *Example*: Fetching object data with a closure:

swift

```swift
func loadObjectData(completion: @escaping (ObjectData) -> Void) {

    // Load data asynchronously

    completion(fetchedData)

}
```

- **Grand Central Dispatch (GCD) for Background Processing**: GCD is essential for running tasks on background threads, preventing the app's main thread from slowing down. In AR, GCD can be used for performance-intensive tasks, like image processing or physics calculations.

- ○ *Example*: Performing background tasks with GCD:

swift

```
DispatchQueue.global(qos: .userInitiated).async {

    // Background task

    DispatchQueue.main.async {

        // Update UI on main thread

    }

}
```

4.3.4 Structuring for Readability: Naming Conventions and Comments

- **Descriptive Naming Conventions**: Swift encourages descriptive naming for variables, functions, and classes, making code more readable. Using names that clearly describe each element's purpose helps others (or future you) quickly understand your code.

  - ○ *Example*: Naming an AR object setup function:

swift

```
func initializeVirtualCube(with color: UIColor) ->
SCNBox { /* code */ }
```

- **Commenting for Clarity**: Clear, concise
  comments provide context and describe the
  purpose of complex sections of code, especially
  in AR applications where interactions may
  involve multiple layers of abstraction.
  Commenting each major section or function
  clarifies code flow for collaborators and future
  edits.

Chapter 5: Understanding 3D Space and Coordinate Systems

5.1 Basics of 3D Space: Coordinate Systems and Object Placement

5.1.1 Introduction to 3D Coordinate Systems

- **The Cartesian Coordinate System**: 3D space in ARKit is based on the Cartesian coordinate system, using three perpendicular axes: X, Y, and Z. Understanding this system is foundational, as it defines how objects are positioned and manipulated in AR.

    - *X-Axis*: Runs horizontally, usually representing the left-to-right orientation.

    - *Y-Axis*: Runs vertically, often representing the up-and-down orientation.

    - *Z-Axis*: Runs perpendicularly to the X-Y plane, representing the forward-and-backward orientation.

- **Positioning Objects in 3D Space**: Each point in 3D space is defined by coordinates (x, y, z). In AR, these coordinates determine an object's position relative to the origin, typically located at the device's starting position.

  - *Example*: Placing an object at (0, 0, -0.5) means it's half a meter in front of the user.

5.1.2 Local vs. World Coordinate Systems

- **Local Coordinate System**: This refers to the coordinate system within a specific object's space. When an object is created, its origin (0,0,0) is typically at the center of the object, allowing for relative positioning and transformations within the object itself.

- **World Coordinate System**: The global coordinate system in which all objects are positioned relative to the AR scene. This system allows objects to be anchored to real-world surfaces or aligned with other objects in a shared space.

  - *Example*: A chair placed in an AR living room scene uses world coordinates to position it in the correct location relative to other furniture.

5.1.3 Understanding Object Placement in ARKit

- **Anchors and Planes**: ARKit uses anchors to fix virtual objects to real-world surfaces. Anchors can detect flat surfaces (like tables or floors) and attach virtual objects to these planes. This helps AR objects appear stable and part of the environment.

- **Placing Objects with SceneKit or RealityKit**: Using SceneKit or RealityKit, developers can specify object coordinates, allowing precise placement within the AR scene. ARKit's coordinate system ensures objects stay fixed even as users move their devices.

5.2 Orientation, Positioning, and Scaling in ARKit

5.2.1 Orientation in 3D Space

- **Understanding Orientation with Euler Angles**: Orientation in 3D space can be defined using Euler angles, which specify rotations along each axis (pitch, yaw, and roll). In ARKit, orientation is particularly relevant for aligning objects to match real-world perspectives.

  - *Pitch*: Rotation around the X-axis, controlling the object's up or down tilt.

  - *Yaw*: Rotation around the Y-axis, controlling the object's left or right turn.

- *Roll*: Rotation around the Z-axis, controlling the object's tilt side-to-side.

- *Example*: If you want to rotate an object to face the user, you might set its yaw angle to match the device's orientation.

- **Using Quaternions for Smooth Rotations**: Quaternions provide a more advanced way to manage rotations in 3D space, avoiding gimbal lock (a condition where multiple axis rotations become indistinguishable). ARKit uses quaternions for smoother, more accurate orientation handling.

5.2.2 Positioning in ARKit with SCNVector3 and Transform Matrices

- **SCNVector3 for Positioning**: SCNVector3 is a class in SceneKit that represents a 3D position vector. It defines an object's position in terms of X, Y, and Z coordinates. In ARKit, SCNVector3 can set an object's location relative to the world or to other objects.

  - *Example*: SCNVector3(x: 0, y: 0.1, z: -0.5) places an object 10 centimeters above and half a meter in front of the device.

- **Transform Matrices for Complex Translations**: Transform matrices allow developers to translate (move), rotate, and scale objects using mathematical operations. In

ARKit, they are essential for handling interactions that involve multiple simultaneous changes in position or rotation.

- ○ *Example*: Applying a transform matrix to move an object in response to a swipe gesture.

5.2.3 Scaling in ARKit

- **Setting Object Scale**: Scale determines the size of an object relative to its original dimensions. In ARKit, scaling is applied using an SCNVector3, allowing each dimension (X, Y, Z) to be scaled independently.

    - ○ *Example*: Scaling a 3D object by setting objectNode.scale = SCNVector3(1.5, 1.5, 1.5) increases its size by 50% in all directions.

- **Maintaining Realistic Proportions**: Scaling in AR should be proportionate to other objects in the environment to maintain realism. For instance, a 3D table should be scaled to a size that matches other real-world furniture in the scene.

- **Dynamic Scaling Based on User Interaction**: Dynamic scaling allows users to resize objects through gestures like pinch-to-zoom. Implementing this feature involves handling touch gestures and updating the object's scale property accordingly.

5.3 Practical Exercise: Placing a Virtual Object in Real-World Space

5.3.1 Setting Up the AR Session

- **Creating an AR Configuration**: Start by creating an ARWorldTrackingConfiguration to allow ARKit to track the device's movement and map the environment. This configuration enables plane detection and light estimation, essential for realistic object placement.

  - *Code Example*:

swift

```
let configuration = ARWorldTrackingConfiguration()

configuration.planeDetection = [.horizontal]

arView.session.run(configuration)
```

5.3.2 Adding a Virtual Object to the Scene

- **Creating the 3D Object**: Define a simple 3D shape, such as a box or sphere, using SceneKit's geometry classes. This will serve as the virtual object that users can place in the real world.

  - *Code Example*:

swift

```swift
let box = SCNBox(width: 0.1, height: 0.1, length: 0.1,
chamferRadius: 0)
```

```swift
let boxNode = SCNNode(geometry: box)
```

```swift
boxNode.position = SCNVector3(0, 0, -0.5) // Place it
half a meter in front
```

- **Customizing the Object's Appearance**: Set
  properties like color, texture, or material to
  make the object visually engaging. This can be
  achieved by modifying the geometry's material.

  - *Example*:

swift

```swift
box.firstMaterial?.diffuse.contents = UIColor.red
```

5.3.3 Detecting and Responding to User Input

- **Handling Tap Gestures for Object
  Placement**: Use a tap gesture recognizer to
  detect when a user taps on a detected plane.
  This allows users to place the virtual object on a
  real-world surface of their choice.

  - *Code Example*:

swift

```swift
let tapGesture = UITapGestureRecognizer(target: self,
action: #selector(handleTap(_:)))
```

```swift
arView.addGestureRecognizer(tapGesture)


@objc func handleTap(_ sender:
UITapGestureRecognizer) {

    let location = sender.location(in: arView)

    let hitTestResults = arView.hitTest(location, types:
.existingPlaneUsingExtent)

    if let hitResult = hitTestResults.first {

        placeObject(at: hitResult)

    }

}
```

- **Placing the Object at the Detected Location**:
  Once a plane is detected, place the object at the
  specified coordinates using the hit test result,
  which provides the exact location of the tapped
  area in 3D space.

  o *Code Example*:

swift

```swift
func placeObject(at hitResult: ARHitTestResult) {

    let boxNode = SCNNode(geometry: box)

    boxNode.position = SCNVector3(

        hitResult.worldTransform.columns.3.x,
```

```
        hitResult.worldTransform.columns.3.y,

        hitResult.worldTransform.columns.3.z

    )

    scene.rootNode.addChildNode(boxNode)

}
```

5.3.4 Enhancing Realism with Light and Shadow

- **Enabling Light Estimation**: Use ARKit's light estimation feature to match the lighting conditions in the AR scene with the real world. This adjustment helps make the object appear more integrated into the environment.

    o *Code Example*:

swift

```
if let lightEstimate =
arView.session.currentFrame?.lightEstimate {

    sceneView.scene.lightingEnvironment.intensity =
lightEstimate.ambientIntensity / 1000

}
```

- **Adding Shadows to the Object**: Apply shadow properties to the 3D object's material to give it a more grounded appearance. This can be done by setting shadow attributes on the object's node or on the light source in the scene.

o *Code Example*:

swift

boxNode.castsShadow = true

sceneView.autoenablesDefaultLighting = true

5.3.5 Testing and Refining Object Placement

- **Testing on Real Devices**: Run the app on an iOS device to observe how the object behaves when placed in real-world space. Test in different lighting conditions and on various surfaces to ensure accurate placement.

- **Refining Object Placement**: Adjust the object's orientation, scale, and interaction settings to achieve a more realistic look. For instance, tweak the object's size if it appears too large or small relative to other objects in the environment.

Chapter 6: Building Interactive AR Scenes with SceneKit

6.1 Basics of SceneKit for 3D Object Rendering

6.1.1 What is SceneKit?

- **Introduction to SceneKit**: SceneKit is Apple's high-level 3D graphics framework for creating, animating, and rendering 3D content on iOS, macOS, and tvOS. It's especially compatible with ARKit, making it a popular choice for AR development.

- **Why SceneKit for AR?**: SceneKit simplifies adding 3D objects and animations to AR applications. It provides intuitive classes and tools for handling 3D geometry, materials, lighting, and cameras without requiring extensive 3D graphics expertise.

6.1.2 Key SceneKit Concepts and Classes

- **SCNNode**: SCNNode represents a position in 3D space and serves as the container for SceneKit objects. Nodes can hold various properties (position, rotation, scale) and be parented to each other to create complex object hierarchies.

- **SCNGeometry**: SCNGeometry defines the shape or structure of a 3D object. Common geometries include SCNBox, SCNSphere, SCNCylinder, and SCNPlane, which are ideal for creating basic 3D shapes in AR.

- **SCNScene**: SCNScene represents the entire 3D space and serves as the container for all nodes, lights, and cameras. In ARKit, the ARSCNView class is used to embed SCNScene within an AR session, displaying it to the user in augmented reality.

6.1.3 Setting Up SceneKit with ARKit

- **ARSCNView**: ARSCNView is a specialized SCNView that integrates ARKit capabilities with SceneKit. It allows developers to render AR content, manage camera input, and utilize AR session data seamlessly.

  - *Example Code*: Initializing ARSCNView in Swift:

swift

```
let sceneView = ARSCNView(frame: self.view.frame)
self.view.addSubview(sceneView)
let scene = SCNScene()
```

```swift
sceneView.scene = scene

sceneView.autoenablesDefaultLighting = true
```

- **Configuring the AR Session**: To enable AR functionality, configure an ARWorldTrackingConfiguration for the AR session. This allows for accurate tracking of the device's position and orientation in 3D space.

  - *Example Code*:

swift

```swift
let configuration = ARWorldTrackingConfiguration()

configuration.planeDetection = [.horizontal, .vertical]

sceneView.session.run(configuration)
```

6.2 Adding Lights, Textures, and Colors to 3D Objects

6.2.1 Working with Lights in SceneKit

- **Types of Lights in SceneKit**: SceneKit offers various light types, including ambient, directional, omni, and spot. Each serves a distinct purpose in creating realistic lighting effects.

- o *Ambient Light*: Provides uniform lighting in all directions, simulating indirect light.

- o *Omni Light*: Radiates light in all directions from a single point, similar to a lightbulb.

- o *Directional Light*: Projects light uniformly in a specific direction, simulating sunlight.

- o *Spot Light*: Casts a cone-shaped light beam, ideal for focusing light on specific areas.

- **Adding Lights to a Scene**: Lights are added by creating SCNLight objects and attaching them to SCNNode. Adjust properties like intensity, color, and shadow settings to control the light's appearance.

  - o *Example Code*: Adding directional light to a scene.

swift

```
let lightNode = SCNNode()

let light = SCNLight()

light.type = .directional

light.intensity = 1000

light.color = UIColor.white
```

```swift
lightNode.light = light

lightNode.position = SCNVector3(x: 0, y: 10, z: 10)

scene.rootNode.addChildNode(lightNode)
```

6.2.2 Applying Textures and Materials to 3D Objects

- **Understanding Materials in SceneKit**: SCNMaterial defines the appearance of 3D objects. By modifying its properties, developers can adjust the object's color, reflectivity, texture, and more.

  - *Diffuse*: The basic color or texture applied to the object's surface.

  - *Specular*: Controls the shininess or reflectiveness, which is useful for simulating metals or polished surfaces.

  - *Normal Map*: Adds surface detail to simulate textures like bumps or grooves.

- **Using Textures for Realism**: Textures can be applied to the diffuse property of SCNMaterial to give the object a realistic appearance. SceneKit supports various image formats, allowing for high-quality textures.

  - *Example Code*: Applying a texture to a 3D object.

swift

```swift
let material = SCNMaterial()

material.diffuse.contents = UIImage(named:
"wood_texture.jpg")

box.geometry?.materials = [material]
```

6.2.3 Adding Colors to Objects

- **Setting Basic Colors**: Colors can be easily
  added to SCNMaterial's diffuse property,
  allowing for simple customization of 3D objects
  without textures.

    - *Example Code*: Setting a solid color for
      an object.

swift

```swift
let material = SCNMaterial()

material.diffuse.contents = UIColor.blue

cubeNode.geometry?.materials = [material]
```

- **Combining Colors with Textures**: SceneKit
  allows combining color and texture effects,
  making it possible to create unique appearances,
  such as semi-transparent or metallic finishes by
  modifying properties like transparency and
  specular.

6.3 Example Project: Designing a Basic AR Scene

6.3.1 Creating the AR Scene with SceneKit

- **Initializing ARSCNView and Configuring the Session**: Start by creating an ARSCNView and configuring an ARWorldTrackingConfiguration. Enable plane detection to anchor objects on real-world surfaces.

  o *Code Example*:

swift

```
let sceneView = ARSCNView(frame: self.view.frame)

self.view.addSubview(sceneView)

let configuration = ARWorldTrackingConfiguration()

configuration.planeDetection = .horizontal

sceneView.session.run(configuration)
```

6.3.2 Adding a 3D Object to the Scene

- **Creating and Placing a 3D Object**: Use SceneKit to create a basic 3D object (such as a box or sphere) and add it to the scene's root node. For simplicity, a SCNBox object will be used as the main object in this AR scene.

o *Code Example*:

swift

```
let box = SCNBox(width: 0.2, height: 0.2, length: 0.2,
chamferRadius: 0.02)

let boxNode = SCNNode(geometry: box)

boxNode.position = SCNVector3(x: 0, y: 0, z: -0.5)

sceneView.scene.rootNode.addChildNode(boxNode)
```

6.3.3 Adding Lights and Shadows for Realism

- **Creating Ambient Light**: Add ambient light to ensure the object is evenly illuminated, making it more visible in all environments.

- **Adding Directional Light for Shadows**: Adding a directional light to the scene creates realistic shadows for the 3D object, giving the scene depth and making it appear more integrated with the physical environment.

  o *Example Code*:

swift

```
let ambientLight = SCNLight()

ambientLight.type = .ambient

ambientLight.intensity = 500
```

```
let ambientLightNode = SCNNode()

ambientLightNode.light = ambientLight

sceneView.scene.rootNode.addChildNode(ambientLightNode)


let directionalLight = SCNLight()

directionalLight.type = .directional

directionalLight.intensity = 1000

let directionalLightNode = SCNNode()

directionalLightNode.light = directionalLight

directionalLightNode.position = SCNVector3(x: 0, y: 10, z: 10)

sceneView.scene.rootNode.addChildNode(directionalLightNode)
```

6.3.4 Adding Interactivity: Tap Gesture for Object Manipulation

- **Implementing a Tap Gesture Recognizer**: Add a tap gesture recognizer to allow users to interact with the 3D object by tapping on it. This interaction could, for example, change the object's color or trigger an animation.

- **Handling the Tap Action**: Define an action in the tap gesture recognizer's target function, such as rotating or changing the object's color. This makes the scene interactive and engaging.

- ○ *Example Code*:

swift

```
let tapGesture = UITapGestureRecognizer(target: self,
action: #selector(handleTap(_:)))

sceneView.addGestureRecognizer(tapGesture)


@objc func handleTap(_ sender:
UITapGestureRecognizer) {
    let location = sender.location(in: sceneView)
    let hitResults = sceneView.hitTest(location, options:
nil)
    if let hitResult = hitResults.first {
        let node = hitResult.node
        node.geometry?.materials.first?.diffuse.contents =
UIColor.random() // Changes color
    }
}
```

6.3.5 Testing and Refining the Scene

- **Running the Project on an AR-Enabled Device**: Test the AR scene on an AR-capable iOS device to observe how the object appears in real-world space. Check for lighting, positioning, and responsiveness to ensure the object feels naturally integrated.

- **Adjusting Parameters for Realism**: Fine-tune parameters such as lighting intensity, object scale, and material properties based on testing results. Adjustments may include refining light angles or making the object more or less transparent.

Chapter 7: User Interaction in AR Applications

7.1 Understanding and Implementing Touch and Gesture Recognizers

7.1.1 Introduction to Gesture Recognizers in AR

- **Role of Gesture Recognizers in AR**: Gesture recognizers are a crucial tool in AR applications, allowing users to interact with virtual objects using familiar touch gestures like taps, swipes, pinches, and rotations. In AR, gesture recognizers enhance immersion by enabling intuitive, real-time interactions with 3D content.

- **Types of Gesture Recognizers**: Common gesture recognizers include:

    - **Tap**: Detects a quick tap on the screen, often used to select or place an object.

    - **Pan/Swipe**: Detects dragging or swiping motions, useful for moving or repositioning objects in AR.

- o **Pinch**: Detects two-finger pinching motions, typically used for scaling (zooming in/out) objects.

- o **Rotation**: Detects rotation gestures, allowing users to spin or rotate objects in 3D space.

7.1.2 Implementing Gesture Recognizers in Swift

- **Setting Up Gesture Recognizers in ARSCNView**: Gesture recognizers can be added to ARSCNView, the view responsible for displaying AR content, allowing users to interact with objects in the scene.

- **Tap Gesture Recognizer**: A tap gesture recognizer is ideal for selecting objects, changing colors, or placing objects in the AR scene.

  - o *Example Code*:

swift

```swift
let tapGesture = UITapGestureRecognizer(target: self,
action: #selector(handleTap(_:)))

sceneView.addGestureRecognizer(tapGesture)


@objc func handleTap(_ sender:
UITapGestureRecognizer) {
```

```swift
let location = sender.location(in: sceneView)

let hitTestResults = sceneView.hitTest(location,
options: nil)

if let hitResult = hitTestResults.first {

    let node = hitResult.node

    node.geometry?.materials.first?.diffuse.contents =
UIColor.random()

    }

}
```

- **Pinch Gesture Recognizer**: A pinch gesture recognizer is useful for scaling objects in AR. By adjusting an object's scale based on the pinch gesture's properties, users can resize objects intuitively.

    o *Example Code*:

swift


```swift
let pinchGesture = UIPinchGestureRecognizer(target:
self, action: #selector(handlePinch(_:)))

sceneView.addGestureRecognizer(pinchGesture)


@objc func handlePinch(_ sender:
UIPinchGestureRecognizer) {
```

```swift
guard let node = selectedNode else { return }

let pinchScaleX = Float(sender.scale) * node.scale.x

let pinchScaleY = Float(sender.scale) * node.scale.y

let pinchScaleZ = Float(sender.scalc) * node.scale.z

node.scale = SCNVector3(pinchScaleX,
pinchScaleY, pinchScaleZ)

sender.scale = 1

}
```

- **Pan Gesture Recognizer**: A pan gesture recognizer is used to move objects around the AR scene, simulating dragging. By adjusting the object's position relative to the user's touch, pan gestures create smooth, interactive movement.

  o *Example Code*:

swift

```swift
let panGesture = UIPanGestureRecognizer(target: self,
action: #selector(handlePan(_:)))

sceneView.addGestureRecognizer(panGesture)


@objc func handlePan(_ sender:
UIPanGestureRecognizer) {
```

```
let translation = sender.translation(in: sceneView)

let newPosition = SCNVector3(translation.x / 1000,
0, translation.y / 1000)

selectedNode?.position = newPosition
}
```

7.2 Designing User Interfaces (UI) for Immersive AR Experiences

7.2.1 UI Components in AR Applications

- **On-Screen Controls for AR**: Designing UI for AR applications is unique, as the focus is on blending digital content with the real world rather than on traditional screens. Common AR UI elements include:

  o **Buttons**: For actions like capturing screenshots, resetting scenes, or triggering animations.

  o **Sliders**: For adjusting attributes such as scale, opacity, or brightness of virtual objects.

  o **Labels**: Useful for displaying brief information about objects, such as names, descriptions, or measurements.

o **Floating UI Elements**: Panels or icons that follow the user's view can be used for settings or navigation.

- **Minimizing Intrusive UI**: In AR, less is more. Avoid overcrowding the screen with UI elements to maintain immersion. Lightweight, transparent, or hidden UIs (e.g., appearing only when tapped) can keep the focus on the AR content.

7.2.2 Designing Interactive Elements in AR

- **Gesture-Based Controls**: AR applications benefit from gesture-based interactions because they create a more natural, intuitive experience for users. Designing interactions around gestures like tapping to place objects or pinching to resize adds to the realism of the experience.

- **Contextual UI Elements**: Display information or controls only when they're relevant to the current interaction. For example, show object-related options (like rotation or color adjustment) only when an object is selected.

- **Real-World Anchoring**: Anchoring UI elements to real-world objects can make the experience more interactive. For example, displaying information about a chair when the user looks at it or tapping on it to reveal additional options.

7.2.3 Practical Tips for Creating AR UI

- **Use Semi-Transparent UI Elements**: Semi-transparent backgrounds on buttons or sliders prevent distraction and allow users to focus on AR content.

- **Integrate Real-World Contexts**: Keep UI elements relevant to the environment. For instance, use icons or labels that highlight real-world items and respond to user actions within the AR scene.

- **Optimize for Accessibility**: Since AR involves dynamic user movement, ensure that UI elements are large enough to interact with easily, and avoid placing buttons or icons too close to screen edges.

7.3 Real-World Example: Building an Interactive Product Viewer

7.3.1 Setting Up the AR Scene for a Product Viewer

- **Overview of the Product Viewer**: An interactive product viewer lets users place and manipulate 3D models of products in their environment, enabling a try-before-you-buy experience. This feature is particularly useful in retail and e-commerce.

- **Setting Up ARSCNView and Configuration**: Initialize ARSCNView and configure

ARWorldTrackingConfiguration to enable plane detection and world tracking.

    ○   *Code Example*:

swift

```
let sceneView = ARSCNView(frame: self.view.frame)

self.view.addSubview(sceneView)

let configuration = ARWorldTrackingConfiguration()

configuration.planeDetection = .horizontal

sceneView.session.run(configuration)
```

7.3.2 Loading and Placing the Product Model

- **Loading a 3D Product Model**: Use SceneKit's SCNScene to load a 3D model (e.g., a piece of furniture or a decorative item) from a file. The model can be in a .scn or .dae format, which are commonly supported by SceneKit.

    ○   *Code Example*:

swift

```
let productScene = SCNScene(named: "product_model.scn")

let productNode = productScene?.rootNode.clone()
```

```swift
productNode?.position = SCNVector3(0, 0, -0.5) //
Half a meter in front of user
```

```swift
sceneView.scene.rootNode.addChildNode(productNode!)
```

- **Placing the Model on a Real-World Surface**:
  Detect a flat surface and place the product
  model on it. This provides a realistic product
  preview within the user's environment.

  o *Code Example*:

swift

```swift
func placeProduct(at location: CGPoint) {
    let hitTestResults = sceneView.hitTest(location,
types: .existingPlaneUsingExtent)
    if let hitResult = hitTestResults.first {
        productNode.position =
SCNVector3(hitResult.worldTransform.columns.3.x,

hitResult.worldTransform.columns.3.y,

hitResult.worldTransform.columns.3.z)
    }
}
```

7.3.3 Adding Interactive Features for Product Customization

- **Scaling the Product Model with Pinch Gesture**: Implement a pinch gesture recognizer to allow users to resize the product model within the AR scene. This helps users visualize different product sizes to match their space.

- **Rotating the Product Model**: Add a rotation gesture recognizer to allow users to spin or rotate the product model, viewing it from various angles.

  - *Example Code for Rotation*:

swift

```
let rotationGesture =
UIRotationGestureRecognizer(target: self, action:
#selector(handleRotation(_:)))

sceneView.addGestureRecognizer(rotationGesture)


@objc func handleRotation(_ sender:
UIRotationGestureRecognizer) {

    productNode?.eulerAngles.y -=
Float(sender.rotation)

    sender.rotation = 0

}
```

7.3.4 Adding UI Elements for Additional Information

- **Product Information Overlay**: Display information about the product, such as its name, price, or specifications. This can be a simple overlay that appears when the product is tapped.

- **Interactive Color Picker**: If the product has color options, create a color picker UI that allows users to select different colors for the product. Change the product's material based on the selected color.

  o *Example Code for Color Change*:

swift

```
func changeProductColor(to color: UIColor) {

productNode.geometry?.materials.first?.diffuse.contents = color

}
```

7.3.5 Testing and Finalizing the Product Viewer

- **Testing User Interactions**: Run the app on an AR-capable device to ensure the gestures respond as expected. Verify that object placement is accurate, resizing and rotation are smooth, and UI elements are visible yet non-intrusive.

- **Optimizing for Different Environments**: Test the product viewer in various lighting conditions and spaces (e.g., small rooms, larger rooms, outdoor settings) to ensure it behaves consistently across environments.

Chapter 8: Working with Real-World Anchors

8.1 Introduction to AR Anchors and Their Purpose

8.1.1 What are AR Anchors?

- **Definition and Role in AR**: In ARKit, an anchor is a fixed point in the real-world environment that serves as a reference for placing virtual objects. Anchors provide stability and consistency, enabling virtual content to stay in place as the user moves their device. Anchors are crucial for creating immersive and realistic AR experiences, as they link the virtual world to the physical space.

- **How Anchors Work**: When an anchor is created, ARKit calculates its position and orientation within the world's coordinate system, allowing developers to attach virtual objects to these anchors. This ensures that objects appear fixed and don't drift as the device moves.

- **Anchors and World Tracking**: World tracking in ARKit uses the device's camera and motion sensors to detect surfaces, capture depth information, and maintain spatial awareness. Anchors rely on this tracking data to establish their location, helping virtual objects blend seamlessly with the real world.

8.1.2 Why Use Anchors in AR Applications?

- **Consistency of Object Placement**: Anchors maintain the stability of virtual objects, even if the user moves the camera away and returns to the object. This is especially useful in scenarios where objects need to remain in a fixed position, such as placing furniture in a room or adding labels to real-world items.

- **Increased Realism and Immersion**: By linking virtual objects to real-world anchors, AR applications can enhance immersion, making it appear as though virtual elements truly exist in the physical space. For example, a virtual plant can be anchored to a detected surface, appearing to "sit" on a table.

- **Improved User Interaction**: Anchors can facilitate meaningful interactions, like tapping an object to get information or moving closer to inspect it. Anchoring objects also allows for a more natural experience, as the virtual object behaves predictably and remains fixed in place.

8.2 Types of Anchors: Plane, Image, and Object Anchors

8.2.1 Plane Anchors

- **What are Plane Anchors?** Plane anchors detect flat surfaces like floors, tables, and walls. ARKit uses plane detection to identify and create anchors at these surfaces, making them suitable for positioning objects in open spaces.

- **Horizontal and Vertical Planes**: Plane detection can target horizontal surfaces (e.g., floors and tabletops) and vertical surfaces (e.g., walls). This versatility allows developers to place objects in various locations, enhancing the flexibility of AR applications.

- **Implementing Plane Anchors**: To detect horizontal and vertical surfaces, enable plane detection in the ARWorldTrackingConfiguration. ARKit will then continuously search for flat surfaces, adding anchors as they are detected.

  o *Example Code*:

swift

```
let configuration = ARWorldTrackingConfiguration()
```

```
configuration.planeDetection = [.horizontal, .vertical]

sceneView.session.run(configuration)
```

- **Use Cases for Plane Anchors**: Plane anchors are ideal for applications that involve placing objects on flat surfaces, such as interior design tools, furniture preview apps, or any scenario requiring objects to appear grounded.

8.2.2 Image Anchors

- **What are Image Anchors?** Image anchors detect specific images in the real world and use them as reference points for placing virtual content. ARKit can recognize pre-defined images and attach virtual objects or animations to them, making it ideal for creating interactive AR experiences with printed materials.

- **How Image Anchors Work**: Developers provide ARKit with a set of reference images, each with a real-world physical size. When ARKit detects a matching image in the environment, it creates an anchor at that location.

- **Implementing Image Anchors**: Set up an ARReferenceImage array containing the images to be recognized. ARKit will search for these images and create anchors when they're detected.

  - *Example Code*:

swift

```swift
if let imageToTrack =
ARReferenceImage.referenceImages(inGroupNamed:
"AR Resources", bundle: Bundle.main) {

    let configuration =
ARWorldTrackingConfiguration()

    configuration.detectionImages = imageToTrack

    sceneView.session.run(configuration)

}
```

- **Use Cases for Image Anchors**: Image anchors are commonly used in marketing and education, where virtual content can be overlaid on brochures, posters, or books to enhance the experience. For example, a museum app can use image anchors to display additional information when users point their device at a painting.

8.2.3 Object Anchors

- **What are Object Anchors?** Object anchors detect specific 3D objects, such as physical models, sculptures, or everyday items. ARKit can recognize these objects in real-time, creating anchors at their location to attach virtual elements.

- **How Object Anchors Work**: Similar to image anchors, object anchors use a set of reference objects that ARKit compares to objects in the environment. These references are created using Apple's AR Reference Object Scanner, which captures an object's shape and dimensions.

- **Implementing Object Anchors**: Use ARReferenceObject to define reference objects for ARKit to recognize and anchor in the real world. Once an object is detected, ARKit places a virtual anchor at its position.

  o *Example Code*:

swift

```
if let referenceObjects =
ARReferenceObject.referenceObjects(inGroupNamed:
"AR Objects", bundle: Bundle.main) {

    let configuration =
ARWorldTrackingConfiguration()

    configuration.detectionObjects = referenceObjects

    sceneView.session.run(configuration)

}
```

- **Use Cases for Object Anchors**: Object anchors are often used in industrial and retail applications, where virtual content can provide context or instructions about physical objects. For instance, an instructional app might recognize a specific machine part and overlay step-by-step repair instructions.

8.3 Practical Application: Anchoring Virtual Objects to Real-World Surfaces

8.3.1 Setting Up the AR Session for Anchors

- **Configuring ARWorldTrackingConfiguration**: Start by creating an ARWorldTrackingConfiguration with plane detection enabled. This configuration allows ARKit to detect flat surfaces and create anchors at those locations.

  - *Code Example*:

swift

```swift
let configuration = ARWorldTrackingConfiguration()
configuration.planeDetection = [.horizontal]
sceneView.session.run(configuration)
```

8.3.2 Adding Virtual Objects to Detected Anchors

- **Creating the Virtual Object**: Define a 3D model, such as a box or sphere, using SceneKit's geometry classes. This model will represent the virtual object that will be anchored to a detected surface.

  - *Code Example*:

swift

```
let box = SCNBox(width: 0.1, height: 0.1, length: 0.1, chamferRadius: 0.02)

let boxNode = SCNNode(geometry: box)

boxNode.position = SCNVector3(0, 0, -0.5) // Initial position
```

- **Handling the Plane Anchor Detection**: Implement ARKit's renderer(_:didAdd:for:) delegate method to respond when a plane anchor is detected. This method can place the virtual object at the anchor's location, ensuring it remains fixed in place.

  - *Code Example*:

swift

```swift
func renderer(_ renderer: SCNSceneRenderer, didAdd
node: SCNNode, for anchor: ARAnchor) {

    guard let planeAnchor = anchor as? ARPlaneAnchor
else { return }

    let boxNode = createBoxNode()

    boxNode.position =
SCNVector3(planeAnchor.center.x, 0,
planeAnchor.center.z)

    node.addChildNode(boxNode)

}
```

8.3.3 Updating Anchors for Improved Accuracy

- **Tracking Anchor Updates**: As ARKit refines
  its understanding of the environment, it may
  update existing anchors to improve accuracy.
  Implement the renderer(_:didUpdate:for:)
  method to adjust the virtual object's position if
  the anchor's location or orientation changes.

  - *Code Example*:

swift

```swift
func renderer(_ renderer: SCNSceneRenderer,
didUpdate node: SCNNode, for anchor: ARAnchor) {

    guard let planeAnchor = anchor as? ARPlaneAnchor
else { return }
```

```
        node.position = SCNVector3(planeAnchor.center.x,
0, planeAnchor.center.z)

}
```

- **Maintaining Realism with Anchor Updates**:
  Ensuring virtual objects stay aligned with
  updated anchors is crucial for realism.
  Adjustments to position, rotation, or scale based
  on updated anchor data help prevent objects
  from appearing to float or drift.

8.3.4 Real-World Example: Placing a Virtual Object on a Table

- **Objective**: Create an AR application that
  detects a table as a horizontal plane and places a
  virtual lamp on it. The lamp should remain in
  place even if the user moves around or the
  camera view changes.

- **Step 1: Detect the Table Surface**: Configure
  ARWorldTrackingConfiguration to detect
  horizontal planes and start the AR session.
  ARKit will recognize the table surface and
  create a plane anchor at its location.

- **Step 2: Place the Lamp Model at the Anchor**:
  When a plane anchor is detected, position the
  virtual lamp at the anchor's center, setting it to
  "sit" on the table. Adjust the lamp's height as
  necessary to avoid clipping through the table.

- **Step 3: Test and Refine Placement**: Run the app on an AR-capable device, pointing it at a table. Verify that the lamp stays in place and appears realistic, even as you move the camera around.

  - *Example Code for Lamp Placement*:

swift

```swift
func renderer(_ renderer: SCNSceneRenderer, didAdd node: SCNNode, for anchor: ARAnchor) {

    guard let planeAnchor = anchor as? ARPlaneAnchor else { return }

    let lampNode = createLampNode()

    lampNode.position = SCNVector3(planeAnchor.center.x, planeAnchor.center.y, planeAnchor.center.z)

    node.addChildNode(lampNode)
}


func createLampNode() -> SCNNode {

    let lampGeometry = SCNCylinder(radius: 0.05, height: 0.15)

    let lampNode = SCNNode(geometry: lampGeometry)
```

```
lampGeometry.firstMaterial?.diffuse.contents =
UIColor.yellow

    return lampNode

}
```

8.3.5 Testing and Final Adjustments

- **Testing Object Placement**: Test the app to ensure that the lamp appears correctly positioned and remains stable as you view it from different angles and distances.

- **Optimizing for Realism**: Use additional properties, like shadow casting and light estimation, to increase the realism of the anchored object. Shadows and responsive lighting help the virtual lamp look like it truly belongs on the table.

Chapter 9: Animating AR Objects

9.1 Basics of Animation in AR Using Swift and SceneKit

9.1.1 Understanding SceneKit's Animation Framework

- **Introduction to SceneKit Animations**: SceneKit is Apple's 3D graphics framework that enables animation of virtual objects in AR applications. SceneKit animations allow developers to animate properties like position, rotation, and scale, creating a more dynamic and interactive experience.

- **Why Animation in AR?**: Animations help make AR objects appear lifelike, enhancing immersion by responding visually to user interactions or environmental changes. For example, animating a character to walk on a detected surface or making an object rotate when tapped provides a richer, more engaging experience.

9.1.2 SceneKit Animation Types

- **SCNAction-Based Animations**: SCNAction provides predefined actions that can be combined to create complex animations, such as moving an object along a path, rotating it, or changing its scale. SCNAction is ideal for straightforward animations triggered by user interactions.

- **Keyframe Animations**: Keyframe animations define animations using multiple stages, enabling more complex motions. This is useful when an object needs to follow a specific trajectory or when you want precise control over an animation's flow.

- **Physics-Based Animations**: SceneKit's physics engine allows for realistic simulations, such as objects falling or bouncing, which can be valuable for specific AR applications like games or simulations. Physics-based animations are ideal for interactions with a more realistic look.

9.1.3 Setting Up SceneKit for AR Animations

- **Adding ARSCNView and Configuring the Scene**: Begin by setting up ARSCNView in your view controller and configuring the AR session to support world tracking. This will enable ARKit's real-world tracking, allowing animated objects to appear stable and responsive within the environment.

- ○ *Code Example*:

swift

```
let sceneView = ARSCNView(frame: self.view.frame)

self.view.addSubview(sceneView)

let configuration = ARWorldTrackingConfiguration()

sceneView.session.run(configuration)
```

- **Initializing an Animated Node**: Create an SCNNode that will serve as the object you animate. For example, define a simple 3D object like a cube or sphere that will respond to animations.

- ○ *Code Example*:

swift

```
let cube = SCNBox(width: 0.1, height: 0.1, length: 0.1, chamferRadius: 0.02)

let cubeNode = SCNNode(geometry: cube)

cubeNode.position = SCNVector3(0, 0, -0.5)

sceneView.scene.rootNode.addChildNode(cubeNode)
```

9.2 Key Techniques: Moving, Rotating, and Scaling Objects

9.2.1 Moving Objects with SCNAction

- **Basic Movement Using SCNAction**: Moving an object is achieved with SCNAction.move(to:duration:) or SCNAction.move(by:duration:), which specify either an absolute position or a relative offset. Moving objects can help create animations where AR elements react to user interactions or environment changes.

  o *Example Code*:

swift

```
let moveAction = SCNAction.move(by: SCNVector3(0, 0.2, 0), duration: 1.0)

cubeNode.runAction(moveAction)
```

- **Looping and Repeating Movements**: Use SCNAction.repeatForever(_:) to make an object move continuously, useful for animations like floating or bouncing objects.

  o *Example Code*:

swift

```swift
let upMove = SCNAction.move(by: SCNVector3(0,
0.1, 0), duration: 1.0)

let downMove = SCNAction.move(by: SCNVector3(0,
-0.1, 0), duration: 1.0)

let moveSequence = SCNAction.sequence([upMove,
downMove])

let continuousMove =
SCNAction.repeatForever(moveSequence)

cubeNode.runAction(continuousMove)
```

9.2.2 Rotating Objects

- **Rotating Using SCNAction**:
  SCNAction.rotate(by:around:duration:) allows
  you to rotate objects around a specified axis.
  Rotation is particularly effective for objects like
  virtual globes, characters, or decorative
  elements that need to turn or spin in place.

  - *Example Code*:

swift

```swift
let rotationAction = SCNAction.rotate(by: .pi, around:
SCNVector3(0, 1, 0), duration: 2.0)

cubeNode.runAction(SCNAction.repeatForever(rotatio
nAction))
```

- **Customizing Rotation Animations**: Combine
  rotation actions with easing options (e.g.,

timingMode = .easeInEaseOut) to create smooth, gradual rotations that make the object appear more natural and lifelike.

9.2.3 Scaling Objects

- **Scaling with SCNAction**: SCNAction.scale(by:duration:) changes the size of an object. Scaling can be used to simulate zooming in or out on an object or make it grow or shrink in response to user interactions.

    o *Example Code*:

swift

```
let scaleAction = SCNAction.scale(by: 1.5, duration: 1.0)

cubeNode.runAction(scaleAction)
```

- **Animating Dynamic Scaling with Repeat and Reverse**: To make an object appear to pulse or expand and contract continuously, use a scale action with SCNAction.sequence to combine scaling up and scaling down actions.

    o *Example Code*:

swift

```
let grow = SCNAction.scale(by: 1.5, duration: 0.5)
```

```
let shrink = SCNAction.scale(by: 0.75, duration: 0.5)
```

```
let scaleSequence = SCNAction.sequence([grow, shrink])
```

```
let pulse = SCNAction.repeatForever(scaleSequence)
```

```
cubeNode.runAction(pulse)
```

9.3 Example Project: Animating Objects to Follow User Interactions

9.3.1 Objective of the Project

- **Goal**: Create an interactive AR application where a virtual object (e.g., a sphere or cube) responds to user interactions with different animations. For example, tapping the object will trigger a color change, and pinching will make it grow or shrink, while dragging will move it to a new location.

- **Application Scenario**: This project could be used for interactive product demonstrations or educational apps, where users explore objects in AR by interacting directly with them.

9.3.2 Setting Up the Scene and Objects

- **Configuring the AR Session and SceneView**: Begin by setting up ARSCNView and configuring ARWorldTrackingConfiguration to ensure accurate tracking within the AR environment.

o *Code Example*:

swift

```
let sceneView = ARSCNView(frame: self.view.frame)
self.view.addSubview(sceneView)
let configuration = ARWorldTrackingConfiguration()
configuration.planeDetection = .horizontal
sceneView.session.run(configuration)
```

- **Creating an Interactive Object**: Define a 3D object (e.g., sphere) that users can interact with. Add the object to the scene and set its initial position.

o *Code Example*:

swift

```
let sphere = SCNSphere(radius: 0.05)
let sphereNode = SCNNode(geometry: sphere)
sphereNode.position = SCNVector3(0, 0, -0.5)
sceneView.scene.rootNode.addChildNode(sphereNode)
```

9.3.3 Adding Interaction with Gesture Recognizers

- **Tap Gesture for Color Change**: Use a tap gesture recognizer to detect when the user taps on the object. When tapped, the object will change to a random color using a custom animation.

  o *Code Example*:

swift

```swift
let tapGesture = UITapGestureRecognizer(target: self, action: #selector(handleTap(_:)))

sceneView.addGestureRecognizer(tapGesture)


@objc func handleTap(_ sender: UITapGestureRecognizer) {

    let location = sender.location(in: sceneView)

    let hitTestResults = sceneView.hitTest(location, options: nil)

    if let result = hitTestResults.first, result.node == sphereNode {

        let colorChange = SCNAction.customAction(duration: 0.3) { node, _ in

node.geometry?.materials.first?.diffuse.contents = UIColor.random()
```

```
        }

        sphereNode.runAction(colorChange)

    }

}
```

- **Pinch Gesture for Scaling**: Add a pinch gesture recognizer to allow users to scale the object, increasing or decreasing its size in response to the pinch gesture.

    o *Code Example*:

swift

```
let pinchGesture = UIPinchGestureRecognizer(target:
self, action: #selector(handlePinch(_:)))

sceneView.addGestureRecognizer(pinchGesture)


@objc func handlePinch(_ sender:
UIPinchGestureRecognizer) {

    let scale = Float(sender.scale)

    sphereNode.scale = SCNVector3(scale, scale, scale)

    sender.scale = 1

}
```

- **Pan Gesture for Moving the Object**: Use a pan gesture to let users drag the object across the AR space. The pan gesture updates the object's position based on the user's touch.

- o   *Code Example*:

swift

```
let panGesture = UIPanGestureRecognizer(target: self,
action: #selector(handlePan(_:)))

sceneView.addGestureRecognizer(panGesture)


@objc func handlePan(_ sender:
UIPanGestureRecognizer) {
    let location = sender.location(in: sceneView)
    let hitTestResults = sceneView.hitTest(location,
types: .existingPlaneUsingExtent)
    if let hitResult = hitTestResults.first {
        sphereNode.position =
SCNVector3(hitResult.worldTransform.columns.3.x,

hitResult.worldTransform.columns.3.y,

hitResult.worldTransform.columns.3.z)
    }
}
```

9.3.4 Testing and Refining the Project

- **Testing Interaction and Animation Timing**: Run the app on an AR-compatible device and test each gesture interaction. Confirm that tapping, pinching, and dragging all work smoothly and that the object's animations trigger correctly.

- **Optimizing Animation Flow**: Adjust animation timing, scale factors, and color changes to enhance user experience. Consider using easing options to make animations smoother and more natural.

9.3.5 Enhancing the User Experience

- **Adding Feedback Animations**: Add subtle feedback animations, such as a slight scale-up or pulse when the object is tapped, to make interactions feel more responsive.

- **Using Sound Effects**: Consider adding sound effects or haptic feedback to accompany animations, enhancing the immersive quality of the application.

Chapter 10: Using Physics in AR Environments

10.1 Overview of Physics in AR: Gravity, Collision, and Dynamics

10.1.1 Why Use Physics in AR?

- **Enhancing Realism**: Adding physics makes virtual objects in AR appear and behave more realistically, simulating the effects of real-world forces like gravity and collision. This is essential for applications that aim to blend virtual objects seamlessly into the physical world, creating more immersive experiences.

- **Interactivity and User Engagement**: Physics-based interactions increase user engagement by allowing objects to respond to touches, gestures, and environmental changes. For instance, objects can fall, roll, or bounce, creating a more interactive experience.

- **Applications of Physics in AR**: Common uses include games (where virtual objects interact or collide), educational simulations (demonstrating concepts like force and momentum), and practical applications (like furniture apps that display how pieces react to gravity).

10.1.2 Key Components of Physics in SceneKit

- **SCNPhysicsBody**: This is the core class in SceneKit's physics engine, responsible for defining an object's physical properties, such as mass, velocity, and collision detection. SCNPhysicsBody can be static, dynamic, or kinematic:

  - *Static*: Fixed objects, like floors or walls, which can interact with other objects but do not move.

  - *Dynamic*: Objects affected by physical forces (like gravity) that can move, collide, and interact with other objects.

  - *Kinematic*: Objects that move according to code but still interact with dynamic objects in a physics-based way.

- **SCNPhysicsWorld**: This is the container for all physics bodies in a SceneKit scene, managing how forces, collisions, and interactions are handled within the AR environment.

- **SCNPhysicsShape**: Represents the physical shape of an object for collision detection. Using a shape that accurately matches the object's geometry is critical for realistic collisions and interactions.

10.1.3 Core Physics Properties: Gravity, Collision, and Dynamics

- **Gravity**: Gravity simulates the force that pulls objects downward. In SceneKit, gravity is applied to all dynamic objects by default, making them fall toward the floor or ground in the AR scene.

- **Collision Detection**: Collision settings define how objects interact when they come into contact. For example, if a virtual ball hits a virtual wall, the collision behavior dictates how the ball will bounce off or stop.

- **Friction, Damping, and Restitution**: Additional physics properties, such as friction (resistance to sliding), damping (resistance to motion), and restitution (bounciness), enable fine-tuning for realistic interactions. These properties help simulate materials and create lifelike reactions when objects collide or move.

10.2 Applying Physics to 3D Objects for Realism

10.2.1 Adding Physics Bodies to SceneKit Objects

- **Creating Physics-Enabled Objects**: To apply physics, assign an SCNPhysicsBody to an object, defining its physical properties. For example, to create a dynamic ball that responds to gravity and collisions:

- ○ *Example Code*:

swift

```
let ballGeometry = SCNSphere(radius: 0.05)
let ballNode = SCNNode(geometry: ballGeometry)
ballNode.physicsBody = SCNPhysicsBody(type: .dynamic, shape: nil)
ballNode.physicsBody?.mass = 0.5 // Adjust mass as needed
sceneView.scene.rootNode.addChildNode(ballNode)
```

- **Adjusting Physical Properties**: Modify properties like mass, friction, and restitution to customize the behavior of the object. For example, a heavier mass makes the object respond more realistically to gravity, while a high restitution makes it bouncier.

- ○ *Example Code*:

swift

```
ballNode.physicsBody?.friction = 0.5
ballNode.physicsBody?.restitution = 0.8
```

10.2.2 Using Physics Shapes for Accurate Collisions

- **Creating Custom Physics Shapes**:
  SCNPhysicsShape provides precise control over
  how an object detects collisions. A physics
  shape can match the geometry of the object
  (e.g., box, sphere) or use a simpler
  approximation for improved performance.

  o *Example Code*:

swift

```
let shape = SCNPhysicsShape(geometry:
ballGeometry, options: nil)

ballNode.physicsBody = SCNPhysicsBody(type:
.dynamic, shape: shape)
```

- **Applying Shape Options**: Customize the
  collision shape using options like
  .concavePolyhedron for complex objects or
  .boundingBox for simpler collision detection.
  This ensures that interactions and collisions are
  realistic.

10.2.3 Managing Collision Categories and Bitmasks

- **Collision Categories**: Collision categories enable developers to group objects and define interactions, so certain objects collide while others do not. This is helpful when you want selective interactions between objects, such as allowing a ball to bounce off a wall but pass through other objects.

- **Bitmasks for Collision Control**: Assign bitmasks to objects to filter which collisions are enabled. Set a collision bitmask to specify which categories can interact, and a contact bitmask to detect specific collisions.

  o *Example Code*:

swift

```
ballNode.physicsBody?.categoryBitMask = 1 // Ball category

wallNode.physicsBody?.categoryBitMask = 2 // Wall category

ballNode.physicsBody?.collisionBitMask = 2 // Collide with walls only
```

10.3 Practical Example: Creating a Simple Physics-Based AR Simulation

10.3.1 Project Overview

- **Objective**: Create an AR application where virtual balls drop from above and interact with a virtual floor and walls, simulating a realistic physics environment. The balls should fall under gravity, bounce on collision, and respond to user interactions.

- **Application Scenario**: This project demonstrates physics-based interactions, useful for educational AR experiences, interactive simulations, or AR games where users can manipulate or observe real-world physics in a virtual setting.

10.3.2 Setting Up the Scene with a Physics Floor

- **Configuring the AR Session and SceneView**: Set up an ARSCNView and configure ARWorldTrackingConfiguration for plane detection, allowing the virtual floor to align with a real-world surface.

    o *Code Example*:

swift

```swift
let sceneView = ARSCNView(frame: self.view.frame)
self.view.addSubview(sceneView)
let configuration = ARWorldTrackingConfiguration()
configuration.planeDetection = .horizontal
```

```swift
sceneView.session.run(configuration)
```

- **Adding a Floor with Physics Properties**:
  Create a floor plane and set it as a static physics
  body. The floor serves as a collision surface for
  the balls.

  - *Code Example*:

swift

```swift
let floorGeometry = SCNPlane(width: 1.0, height: 1.0)

let floorNode = SCNNode(geometry: floorGeometry)

floorNode.eulerAngles.x = -.pi / 2 // Lay the plane flat

floorNode.physicsBody = SCNPhysicsBody(type: .static, shape: nil)

floorNode.physicsBody?.friction = 1.0

sceneView.scene.rootNode.addChildNode(floorNode)
```

10.3.3 Creating and Dropping Balls with Physics

- **Adding a Ball with Dynamic Physics**: Define
  a ball node with dynamic physics properties,
  allowing it to fall under gravity and interact
  with the floor.

  - *Code Example*:

swift

```swift
let ballGeometry = SCNSphere(radius: 0.05)

let ballNode = SCNNode(geometry: ballGeometry)

ballNode.position = SCNVector3(0, 0.2, 0) // Start above the floor

ballNode.physicsBody = SCNPhysicsBody(type: .dynamic, shape: nil)

ballNode.physicsBody?.mass = 0.5

ballNode.physicsBody?.restitution = 0.6 // Bounciness

sceneView.scene.rootNode.addChildNode(ballNode)
```

- **Using Tap Gesture to Drop Balls**: Implement a tap gesture recognizer to spawn and drop a new ball each time the user taps the screen. This adds interactivity and allows users to create multiple objects in the scene.

  - *Code Example*:

swift

```swift
let tapGesture = UITapGestureRecognizer(target: self, action: #selector(handleTap(_:)))

sceneView.addGestureRecognizer(tapGesture)


@objc func handleTap(_ sender: UITapGestureRecognizer) {
```

```swift
let ballNode = createBallNode()

ballNode.position = SCNVector3(0, 0.5, 0) // Drop from above

sceneView.scene.rootNode.addChildNode(ballNode)
}
```

10.3.4 Adding Walls for Collision Interaction

- **Creating Walls with Static Physics Bodies**: Define wall nodes with static physics bodies to contain the balls within the scene, providing surfaces for collisions. Place walls around the floor to create a closed environment.

  o *Code Example*:

swift

```swift
let wallGeometry = SCNBox(width: 0.02, height: 0.5, length: 1.0, chamferRadius: 0)

let wallNode = SCNNode(geometry: wallGeometry)

wallNode.position = SCNVector3(0.5, 0.25, 0) // Position beside floor

wallNode.physicsBody = SCNPhysicsBody(type: .static, shape: nil)

sceneView.scene.rootNode.addChildNode(wallNode)
```

10.3.5 Customizing Physics Settings for Realism

- **Adjusting Restitution and Friction for Materials**: Modify the friction and restitution properties of the balls and walls to simulate different materials. High restitution makes objects bouncy, while low friction simulates slippery surfaces.

- **Applying Damping for Motion Control**: Damping reduces motion over time, preventing balls from rolling indefinitely and enhancing realism.

  o *Code Example*:

swift

```
ballNode.physicsBody?.angularDamping = 0.5
ballNode.physicsBody?.linearDamping = 0.3
```

10.3.6 Testing and Optimizing the Simulation

- **Testing Physics Behaviors**: Run the app on an AR-capable device and test how the balls fall, bounce, and interact with the floor and walls. Observe for realistic responses to gravity and collisions.

- **Refining Physics Properties**: Adjust the physics properties based on test results. For example, increase the friction if balls slide too easily or adjust the restitution if they bounce too much or too little.

10.3.7 Enhancing the Experience with Realistic Visuals

- **Adding Shadows and Lighting**: Use SceneKit's lighting and shadow features to enhance the realism of the simulation, making the balls appear naturally integrated with the physical environment.

- **Incorporating Sound Effects**: Adding sound effects for collisions or bounces can enhance immersion. Use AVAudioPlayer to play sounds when objects collide, giving the simulation an extra layer of realism.

Chapter 11: Exploring Advanced Object Recognition

11.1 Implementing Image and Object Recognition with ARKit

11.1.1 Introduction to ARKit's Image and Object Recognition Capabilities

- **What is Image and Object Recognition?**:
  Image and object recognition in ARKit allows
  AR applications to recognize and track images
  or 3D objects in the real world. By recognizing
  predefined images (such as logos or posters)
  and 3D objects, ARKit can create anchors at
  their locations, making it possible to overlay
  virtual content in precise alignment with the
  recognized object.

- **Applications in AR**: Recognizing images or
  objects enhances AR experiences in many
  applications, from augmented brochures and
  posters in marketing to interactive museum
  exhibits and object-based learning tools.

11.1.2 Setting Up Image Recognition with ARKit

- **Creating Reference Images**: To recognize images, ARKit requires a set of reference images stored in an ARReferenceImage group. Each image must have an assigned real-world physical size to ensure accurate scaling when detected.

- **Adding Reference Images to AR Resources**: In Xcode, add images to the AR Resources folder and assign a physical size for each image. ARKit will use this size to scale the virtual overlays accurately.

- **Implementing Image Recognition in ARKit**: Load the reference images into an ARWorldTrackingConfiguration and set the detectionImages property to enable image recognition.

  - *Example Code*:

swift

```
if let referenceImages =
ARReferenceImage.referenceImages(inGroupNamed:
"AR Resources", bundle: Bundle.main) {

    let configuration =
ARWorldTrackingConfiguration()

    configuration.detectionImages = referenceImages

    sceneView.session.run(configuration)
```

}

11.1.3 Setting Up Object Recognition with ARKit

- **Creating 3D Object Scans**: For object recognition, ARKit requires ARReferenceObject files, which contain spatial data about the object. These files are created using the AR Reference Object Scanner app or the scanning capabilities in ARKit.

- **Implementing Object Recognition**: Load ARReferenceObject files and add them to the AR session's configuration. When the app detects a matching object in the environment, ARKit will create an anchor, allowing the app to overlay digital content.

  - *Example Code*:

swift

```swift
if let referenceObjects = ARReferenceObject.referenceObjects(inGroupNamed: "AR Objects", bundle: Bundle.main) {

    let configuration = ARWorldTrackingConfiguration()

    configuration.detectionObjects = referenceObjects

    sceneView.session.run(configuration)

}
```

11.1.4 Real-World Constraints of Recognition

- **Image Quality and Lighting**: The quality of the reference image or object can impact detection accuracy. Clear, high-resolution images and well-lit objects improve recognition rates.

- **Physical Size and Distance**: ARKit performs better with larger reference images or objects that have distinct patterns or shapes. Additionally, ARKit's recognition range is limited, so closer distances are generally more reliable for object recognition.

11.2 Using Real-World Objects as Interactive Triggers

11.2.1 Recognizing Objects as Triggers for Virtual Content

- **Interactive Trigger Concept**: By recognizing specific images or objects in the environment, ARKit can use them as triggers for various actions. For example, when a painting is recognized, ARKit can display additional information, or when a product is detected, an animation can start.

- **Implementing Triggers in ARKit**: Once an image or object is recognized, ARKit creates an anchor that serves as a fixed reference point. Virtual content, such as text, images, or 3D models, can be attached to this anchor, allowing it to follow the real-world object's movements.

11.2.2 Customizing the Interaction Based on the Recognized Object

- **Overlaying Content Based on Object Properties**: Customize the overlay or animation based on the properties of the recognized object. For example, if the app recognizes a specific type of product, it could display a 3D model or animated overlay related to that product.

- **Triggering Animations or Audio Feedback**: Recognized objects can trigger animations, sounds, or videos that engage users more deeply. For example, recognizing a book cover could trigger an animated book opening effect, and recognizing a landmark could trigger audio with historical details.

- **Example Code for Triggered Response**:

swift

```swift
func renderer(_ renderer: SCNSceneRenderer, didAdd
node: SCNNode, for anchor: ARAnchor) {
    if let imageAnchor = anchor as? ARImageAnchor {
```

```
    let overlayNode = createOverlayNode(for:
imageAnchor.referenceImage)

    node.addChildNode(overlayNode)

  }

}


func createOverlayNode(for referenceImage:
ARReferenceImage) -> SCNNode {

  let overlay = SCNPlane(width:
referenceImage.physicalSize.width, height:
referenceImage.physicalSize.height)

  overlay.firstMaterial?.diffuse.contents =
UIImage(named: "OverlayImage")

  return SCNNode(geometry: overlay)

}
```

11.2.3 Enhancing Interactivity with Gesture Recognition

- **Adding Gesture Recognizers to Interact with Recognized Objects**: Once an object is recognized, gesture recognizers (such as tap, pinch, or swipe) can enhance interactivity, allowing users to interact with the virtual content. For example, tapping on an overlaid model could provide more details, while pinching could resize the model.

- **Responding to Gestures Based on Context**: Tailor the interaction based on the specific object being recognized. For example, if the app recognizes a specific animal model, swiping could trigger animations or rotations that give users different views of the model.

11.3 Real-World Application: Designing an AR App that Recognizes and Reacts to Objects

11.3.1 Application Overview

- **Objective**: Create an AR application that recognizes real-world objects (such as a product or artwork) and reacts by displaying relevant virtual content, such as an overlay or an animation. Users can interact with the virtual content through gestures.

- **Application Scenario**: This application could serve various industries, such as retail (where a product triggers an interactive 3D model or description) or education (where an object triggers educational content or animations).

11.3.2 Configuring Image and Object Recognition for the App

- **Setting Up Reference Images and Objects**: Prepare reference images and 3D object scans for items the app will recognize. These could include images of product packaging or scanned models of educational objects.

- **Enabling Image and Object Detection**: Load the reference images and objects into the AR session configuration, enabling ARKit to detect them during the AR experience.

  - *Code Example*:

swift

```
if let referenceImages =
ARReferenceImage.referenceImages(inGroupNamed:
"Product Images", bundle: Bundle.main),

  let referenceObjects =
ARReferenceObject.referenceObjects(inGroupNamed:
"3D Objects", bundle: Bundle.main) {

  let configuration =
ARWorldTrackingConfiguration()

    configuration.detectionImages = referenceImages

    configuration.detectionObjects = referenceObjects

    sceneView.session.run(configuration)

}
```

11.3.3 Creating and Attaching Virtual Overlays

- **Defining Overlays for Recognized Items**: Create overlays or 3D models specific to each item the app will recognize. For example, if the app recognizes a branded product, the overlay could include a promotional animation or 3D model of the product.

- **Attaching Overlays to Anchors**: When ARKit detects an item, attach the corresponding overlay to its anchor, ensuring it follows the item's position and orientation.

  - *Code Example for Overlay Attachment*:

swift

```swift
func renderer(_ renderer: SCNSceneRenderer, didAdd node: SCNNode, for anchor: ARAnchor) {
    if let imageAnchor = anchor as? ARImageAnchor {
        let productOverlay = createProductOverlay(for: imageAnchor.referenceImage)
        node.addChildNode(productOverlay)
    } else if let objectAnchor = anchor as? ARObjectAnchor {
        let objectOverlay = createObjectOverlay(for: objectAnchor.referenceObject)
        node.addChildNode(objectOverlay)
    }
}
```

```swift
func createProductOverlay(for referenceImage:
ARReferenceImage) -> SCNNode {

    let overlayGeometry = SCNPlane(width:
referenceImage.physicalSize.width, height:
referenceImage.physicalSize.height)

    overlayGeometry.firstMaterial?.diffuse.contents =
UIImage(named: "ProductInfoOverlay")

    let overlayNode = SCNNode(geometry:
overlayGeometry)

    overlayNode.eulerAngles.x = -.pi / 2 // Adjust
orientation

    return overlayNode

}
```

11.3.4 Adding Gesture-Based Interactions for Recognized Objects

- **Tap Gesture for Interactive Actions**: Add a tap gesture recognizer to allow users to interact with the virtual content overlaid on recognized items. For example, tapping a recognized object could reveal additional information, start an animation, or change the object's appearance.

    o *Example Code*:

swift

```swift
let tapGesture = UITapGestureRecognizer(target: self,
action: #selector(handleTapOnOverlay(_:)))

sceneView.addGestureRecognizer(tapGesture)


@objc func handleTapOnOverlay(_ sender:
UITapGestureRecognizer) {
    let location = sender.location(in: sceneView)

    let hitTestResults = sceneView.hitTest(location,
options: nil)

    if let result = hitTestResults.first {

        handleInteraction(for: result.node)

    }

}


func handleInteraction(for node: SCNNode) {
    // Perform interaction, e.g., show details, play
animation

    let scaleUp = SCNAction.scale(by: 1.2, duration:
0.2)

    let scaleDown = SCNAction.scale(by: 0.8, duration:
0.2)

    node.runAction(SCNAction.sequence([scaleUp,
scaleDown]))
```

}

11.3.5 Testing and Refining the AR App

- **Testing Object Recognition Accuracy**: Run the app on an AR-capable device, testing recognition accuracy in different lighting conditions and distances. Ensure that the overlay appears as expected and aligns correctly with recognized objects.

- **Refining Overlays and Interactions**: Adjust the positioning and size of overlays to achieve accurate alignment. Test gestures to ensure they trigger actions reliably, and refine animations or interactions as needed.

11.3.6 Enhancing the Experience with Audio and Haptics

- **Adding Sound Effects for Recognized Items**: Use sound effects to provide additional feedback when items are recognized or when users interact with overlays. For example, playing a sound when a product is recognized can make the experience more immersive.

- **Implementing Haptic Feedback**: On supported devices, add haptic feedback to gestures, enhancing the tactile experience of interacting with virtual content.

Chapter 12: Lighting and Shadows for Realism

12.1 Understanding AR Lighting: Ambient and Directional Light

12.1.1 The Role of Lighting in AR

- **Why Lighting Matters in AR**: Lighting plays a crucial role in blending virtual objects into real environments. Correctly applied lighting helps virtual objects look natural, making them appear as if they belong in the physical world. This is essential for creating immersive experiences where users feel like virtual objects are truly part of their surroundings.

- **Types of Lighting in AR**: Different types of lighting in AR help simulate various lighting conditions, from soft, even lighting to intense, focused light. In AR applications, ambient and directional lighting are commonly used to achieve realistic effects.

12.1.2 Ambient Light in AR

- **What is Ambient Light?** Ambient light
  provides even illumination across the entire
  scene, simulating indirect light that bounces off
  surfaces in a room. In AR, ambient light is
  useful for adding soft lighting to virtual objects
  without casting strong shadows, helping them
  blend in with their surroundings.

- **Creating Ambient Light in SceneKit**:
  SceneKit allows you to add ambient light using
  SCNLight objects with the ambient type.
  Ambient lighting can be adjusted in intensity
  and color to suit different environments.

  - *Example Code for Ambient Light*:

swift

```swift
let ambientLight = SCNLight()

ambientLight.type = .ambient

ambientLight.intensity = 1000

ambientLight.color = UIColor.white

let ambientNode = SCNNode()

ambientNode.light = ambientLight

sceneView.scene.rootNode.addChildNode(ambientNode)
```

12.1.3 Directional Light in AR

- **What is Directional Light?** Directional light simulates sunlight, projecting light uniformly in a specified direction. Unlike ambient light, directional light casts shadows, adding depth and realism to virtual objects in AR. Directional lighting is especially effective for outdoor scenes or scenes requiring defined shadows.

- **Creating Directional Light in SceneKit**: SceneKit's SCNLight type also supports directional light, which can be positioned and rotated to create shadows that align with real-world lighting conditions.

  - *Example Code for Directional Light*:

swift

```
let directionalLight = SCNLight()

directionalLight.type = .directional

directionalLight.intensity = 1000

let directionalNode = SCNNode()

directionalNode.light = directionalLight

directionalNode.eulerAngles = SCNVector3(-Float.pi / 4, 0, 0) // Angle the light

sceneView.scene.rootNode.addChildNode(directionalNode)
```

12.2 Light Estimation for Dynamic Environments

12.2.1 What is Light Estimation?

- **The Purpose of Light Estimation**: Light estimation in ARKit allows virtual objects to respond dynamically to changes in real-world lighting. ARKit uses the device's camera to measure ambient light intensity, adjusting virtual lighting accordingly to create a more realistic effect.

- **How Light Estimation Works**: Light estimation gathers information about the real-world lighting environment, including brightness and color temperature, and applies these properties to virtual objects. This makes objects adapt to varying lighting conditions, such as moving from a bright room to a dim hallway.

12.2.2 Implementing Light Estimation in ARKit

- **Enabling Light Estimation**: Light estimation can be enabled in the AR session configuration, allowing ARKit to analyze the real-world environment and update lighting in real-time.

o *Example Code for Enabling Light Estimation*:

swift

let configuration = ARWorldTrackingConfiguration()

configuration.isLightEstimationEnabled = true

sceneView.session.run(configuration)

- **Applying Light Estimation to Virtual Lighting**: Use ARKit's light estimate data to adjust lighting properties dynamically. For instance, modify the ambient light intensity in the scene to match the real-world lighting detected by ARKit.

  o *Example Code for Dynamic Lighting Update*:

swift

```
func renderer(_ renderer: SCNSceneRenderer,
updateAtTime time: TimeInterval) {

   if let lightEstimate =
sceneView.session.currentFrame?.lightEstimate {

      ambientLight.intensity =
lightEstimate.ambientIntensity
```

```
directionalLight.color = UIColor(white:
lightEstimate.ambientColorTemperature / 6500.0,
alpha: 1.0)

    }

}
```

12.2.3 Practical Considerations for Light Estimation

- **Response to Fast Lighting Changes**: Light estimation may not react instantly to abrupt lighting changes (e.g., turning on or off a light). However, it adapts gradually, maintaining a smooth transition to keep virtual objects looking consistent.

- **Combining Light Estimation with Custom Lighting**: While light estimation provides a good foundation, developers can combine it with custom lighting settings to achieve specific effects. For example, a room with colored lighting might require manual color adjustments to match the desired visual tone.

12.3 Enhancing Realism with Shadows: Practical Application

12.3.1 Why Shadows Are Important in AR

- **Shadows for Depth and Realism**: Shadows anchor virtual objects in the real world, adding depth and context by simulating how light interacts with surfaces. Without shadows, virtual objects appear to float, breaking immersion and making them seem out of place.

- **Types of Shadows in SceneKit**: SceneKit supports real-time shadows cast by virtual light sources. Shadows can be adjusted for softness and intensity to align with the scene's requirements.

12.3.2 Creating Shadows in SceneKit

- **Enabling Shadows for Light Sources**: To cast shadows, set a virtual light's shadow-related properties, such as castsShadow, shadowColor, and shadowRadius. Shadows from directional lights are particularly useful for creating realistic effects in AR.

  - *Example Code for Shadows*:

swift

```
directionalLight.castsShadow = true

directionalLight.shadowColor =
UIColor.black.withAlphaComponent(0.5)

directionalLight.shadowRadius = 10
```

12.3.3 Adding Shadow-Casting Objects in AR

- **Adding a Ground Plane for Shadows**: Virtual objects need a surface to cast shadows on, typically a plane that represents the floor or ground. Adding a semi-transparent plane below virtual objects allows shadows to appear as if they're cast on the actual surface.

- **Aligning Shadows with Real-World Lighting**: Position the light source and adjust shadow properties to match the direction and intensity of real-world lighting. For example, if light is coming from a window on the left side of the scene, angle the virtual light source similarly.

  o *Example Code for Ground Plane*:

swift

```
let shadowPlane = SCNPlane(width: 1.0, height: 1.0)
shadowPlane.firstMaterial?.colorBufferWriteMask = []
let planeNode = SCNNode(geometry: shadowPlane)
planeNode.position = SCNVector3(0, 0, -0.5)
sceneView.scene.rootNode.addChildNode(planeNode)
```

12.3.4 Practical Example: Realistic Lighting and Shadows for Virtual Furniture Placement

Step 1: Setting Up the Scene and Lighting

- **Configuring Lighting for a Virtual Room**: Add ambient and directional lighting to simulate indoor lighting conditions. Directional light should be angled to simulate sunlight or indoor lighting from a particular direction.

  - *Example Code for Configuring Room Lighting*:

swift

```
let ambientLight = SCNLight()

ambientLight.type = .ambient

ambientLight.intensity = 500

let ambientNode = SCNNode()

ambientNode.light = ambientLight

sceneView.scene.rootNode.addChildNode(ambientNode)


let directionalLight = SCNLight()

directionalLight.type = .directional

directionalLight.intensity = 1000

directionalLight.castsShadow = true

let directionalNode = SCNNode()
```

```swift
directionalNode.light = directionalLight

directionalNode.eulerAngles = SCNVector3(-.pi / 3, 0,
0)

sceneView.scene.rootNode.addChildNode(directional
Node)
```

Step 2: Creating a Furniture Model with Shadows

- **Adding a Virtual Furniture Object**: Load a
  3D furniture model and position it in the AR
  scene. Assign a dynamic shadow-casting light
  source to create natural-looking shadows under
  the furniture.

  - *Example Code*:

swift

```swift
let table = SCNBox(width: 0.5, height: 0.05, length:
0.5, chamferRadius: 0)

let tableNode = SCNNode(geometry: table)

tableNode.position = SCNVector3(0, 0, -0.5)

sceneView.scene.rootNode.addChildNode(tableNode)
```

Step 3: Using Light Estimation to Match Room Lighting

- **Dynamically Adjusting Lighting**: Apply light
  estimation to update the ambient and directional

lighting properties in real-time, making the furniture's lighting match the room's ambient light levels.

- o *Example Code for Light Estimation*:

swift

```
func renderer(_ renderer: SCNSceneRenderer,
updateAtTime time: TimeInterval) {

    if let lightEstimate =
sceneView.session.currentFrame?.lightEstimate {

        ambientLight.intensity =
lightEstimate.ambientIntensity

        directionalLight.intensity =
lightEstimate.ambientIntensity / 2

    }

}
```

Step 4: Testing and Fine-Tuning Lighting and Shadows

- **Testing Shadow Alignment**: Run the app on an AR-capable device and observe how the shadows appear under the virtual furniture. Adjust shadow softness and color to create a realistic look that matches the environment.

- **Optimizing Performance with Shadow Settings**: If shadows impact performance, adjust properties like shadowSampleCount and shadowRadius to achieve a balance between realism and efficiency. Softening shadows or reducing sample count can maintain realism while improving frame rates.

12.3.5 Additional Techniques for Enhanced Realism

- **Soft Shadows for Indoor Environments**: Indoor lighting often produces softer shadows, so adjust the shadow radius and sample count to create a diffuse shadow effect. This helps the virtual object appear more integrated in home or office environments.

- **Color Temperature Adjustments**: In environments with warm or cool lighting, adjust the light color temperature to match. For instance, if the room lighting is warm, apply a yellowish hue to the virtual lighting.

Chapter 13: Building an AR Game (Part 1)

13.1 Planning an AR Game: Concept, Design, and User Experience

13.1.1 Defining the Game Concept

- **Choosing a Game Genre**: In AR gaming, certain genres work better than others. Popular genres include virtual shooting, puzzle-solving, exploration, and sports. For this example, we'll focus on building a virtual shooting game, where players shoot at targets that appear in their physical environment.

- **Setting Game Objectives**: Clearly defined objectives give players a sense of purpose. In a shooting game, objectives could include achieving high scores, completing levels within a time limit, or hitting targets with varying levels of difficulty. Decide on the game's purpose to guide the overall design and user experience.

- **Designing Interactions and Feedback**: AR games rely heavily on user interactions, so designing intuitive controls and feedback mechanisms is crucial. Consider including visual cues, sound effects, and haptic feedback (vibrations) for each shot, reload, or level-up.

13.1.2 Designing the Game's Core Elements

- **Game Environment**: Since AR games overlay virtual elements onto the real world, it's essential to design environments that are adaptable to various physical spaces. Plan the virtual elements (like targets or obstacles) to fit naturally into a player's surroundings.

- **User Interface (UI) Elements**: In AR games, the UI should be minimal and non-intrusive, so as not to break immersion. Consider adding a score counter, ammo indicator, and level tracker but avoid overcrowding the screen. Place essential UI elements at the screen edges or integrate them into the game environment (e.g., displaying ammo count on the virtual weapon).

- **Virtual Assets**: Decide on the types of objects that will populate the game world. In a shooting game, this could include targets, obstacles, weapons, and environmental elements like walls or barriers that provide cover.

13.1.3 Planning the User Experience (UX)

- **Immersion and Accessibility**: AR games should leverage real-world surroundings for a sense of immersion. Ensure that users can play the game without complex setups or additional hardware. This approach allows for easy access and intuitive gameplay.

- **Creating Engaging Levels**: Design levels that increase in difficulty, adding new challenges or introducing different types of targets and obstacles as players progress. This keeps the gameplay dynamic and engaging.

- **Ensuring Safety in AR Games**: Since players will move around in physical spaces, safety is paramount. Include warnings or prompts for users to be aware of their surroundings to prevent accidental collisions with real-world objects.

13.2 Setting Up the Game's Environment and Elements

13.2.1 Configuring the AR Session

- **Setting Up ARSCNView**: The ARSCNView combines ARKit with SceneKit to render 3D objects in the player's environment. Start by initializing the view and configuring the AR session with plane detection for horizontal surfaces, which will serve as the game's base.

- **Enabling World Tracking**: Use ARWorldTrackingConfiguration for reliable object placement and motion tracking, ensuring a stable game environment.

    o *Example Code*:

swift

```
let sceneView = ARSCNView(frame: self.view.frame)

self.view.addSubview(sceneView)

let configuration = ARWorldTrackingConfiguration()

configuration.planeDetection = .horizontal

sceneView.session.run(configuration)
```

13.2.2 Placing Game Elements in the Real World

- **Using Anchors for Stable Object Placement**: Anchors help virtual objects stay in place, making them appear grounded in the real world. When ARKit detects a plane, use it as an anchor to place targets and obstacles securely within the environment.

- **Creating a Virtual Target**: Define a basic target as an SCNNode with custom geometry (e.g., a sphere or box) or a 3D model. The target will react to user interactions, such as shots, by changing colors, scaling, or disappearing.

swift

```
let targetGeometry = SCNSphere(radius: 0.1)

let targetNode = SCNNode(geometry: targetGeometry)

targetNode.position = SCNVector3(0, 0, -1) // Position
target in front of player

targetNode.name = "target" // Set a name for easy
identification

sceneView.scene.rootNode.addChildNode(targetNode)
```

13.2.3 Defining Weapon and Ammunition Mechanics

- **Weapon Mechanics**: Set up a virtual weapon that players can use to aim and shoot at targets. Use a crosshair or reticle to show where shots will hit, and display an ammo counter that decreases with each shot.

- **Ammunition Logic**: Define the total ammunition and reload mechanics. For example, after 10 shots, the game could prompt the user to reload by tapping a button.

- **Example Code for Ammunition and Firing**:

swift

```swift
var ammoCount = 10

func fireWeapon() {
    if ammoCount > 0 {
        ammoCount -= 1
        shootProjectile()
    } else {
        // Prompt to reload
    }
}
```

13.2.4 Adding Obstacles and Barriers

- **Designing Obstacles**: Obstacles provide variety and make the game more challenging. Add virtual walls or moving barriers that block shots, requiring players to time their actions carefully.

- **Animating Barriers**: Use SCNAction to animate obstacles, making them move up and down or side to side, increasing the difficulty level.

    o *Example Code for Moving Obstacle*:

swift

```
let obstacleGeometry = SCNBox(width: 0.2, height:
0.5, length: 0.1, chamferRadius: 0)

let obstacleNode = SCNNode(geometry:
obstacleGeometry)

obstacleNode.position = SCNVector3(0.5, 0, -1)

let moveUp = SCNAction.move(by: SCNVector3(0,
0.5, 0), duration: 1.0)

let moveDown = SCNAction.move(by:
SCNVector3(0, -0.5, 0), duration: 1.0)

let moveSequence = SCNAction.sequence([moveUp,
moveDown])

obstacleNode.runAction(SCNAction.repeatForever(m
oveSequence))

sceneView.scene.rootNode.addChildNode(obstacleNo
de)
```

13.3 Example Project: Building a Virtual Shooting Game

13.3.1 Setting the Game Objective and Rules

- **Objective**: In this virtual shooting game, the goal is to shoot as many targets as possible within a given time limit. Each target hit increases the score, while missed shots have no penalty.

- **Rules**: Players are given 10 shots per round, and they must reload after depleting their ammo. Points are awarded based on accuracy, and levels increase in difficulty as more targets and moving obstacles appear.

13.3.2 Adding Shooting Mechanics

- **Detecting Hits on Targets**: Implement a tap gesture recognizer to detect when the player "shoots" by tapping the screen. The tap location is then converted into a ray that detects collisions with targets in the AR scene.

- **Triggering Hit Responses**: When a target is hit, it responds by disappearing, playing an animation, or changing color to indicate a successful shot. Update the score for each hit.

  o *Example Code for Shooting Mechanic*:

swift

```
let tapGesture = UITapGestureRecognizer(target: self,
action: #selector(handleTap(_:)))

sceneView.addGestureRecognizer(tapGesture)


@objc func handleTap(_ sender:
UITapGestureRecognizer) {

    let location = sender.location(in: sceneView)
```

```swift
    let hitTestResults = sceneView.hitTest(location,
options: [SCNHitTestOption.searchMode:
SCNHitTestSearchMode.all.rawValue])


    for result in hitTestResults {
        if result.node.name == "target" {
            result.node.removeFromParentNode()
            increaseScore()
        }
    }
}


func increaseScore() {
    // Update score logic
}
```

13.3.3 Implementing Scoring and Feedback

- **Scoring System**: Display a score counter that increases with each target hit. Points could be based on the target's distance from the player or other factors, such as bonus points for hitting multiple targets in quick succession.

- **Visual and Audio Feedback**: Use sound effects and animations to give feedback on successful shots. A simple animation, such as scaling the target briefly before it disappears, adds visual engagement.

    o   *Example Code for Visual Feedback*:

swift

```swift
func provideFeedback(for targetNode: SCNNode) {
    let scaleUp = SCNAction.scale(to: 1.2, duration: 0.1)
    let scaleDown = SCNAction.scale(to: 0, duration: 0.2)
    let sequence = SCNAction.sequence([scaleUp, scaleDown])
    targetNode.runAction(sequence)
}
```

13.3.4 Creating Level Progression and Timers

- **Level Progression**: Design levels that increase in difficulty, adding more targets or faster-moving obstacles as the player progresses. After hitting a certain number of targets, the player advances to the next level.

- **Adding a Timer**: Set a time limit for each level, encouraging players to act quickly. Display a countdown timer in the corner of the screen, and end the game when time runs out.

swift

```swift
var timeRemaining = 60

func startTimer() {
    Timer.scheduledTimer(withTimeInterval: 1.0,
repeats: true) { timer in
        self.timeRemaining -= 1
        if self.timeRemaining == 0 {
            timer.invalidate()
            self.endGame()
        }
    }
}


func endGame() {
    // End game logic
}
```

13.3.5 Testing and Refining the Game Mechanics

- **Testing on AR-Compatible Devices**: Run the game on an AR-compatible device, testing different levels and player interactions. Ensure that targets, obstacles, and weapon mechanics function smoothly.

- **Adjusting Difficulty and Gameplay Balance**: Tweak factors like target speed, obstacle behavior, and reload timing to create a balanced and engaging experience. Adjust levels to maintain the game's challenge while keeping it fun and fair.

Chapter 14: Building an AR Game (Part 2)

14.1 Adding Interactivity: User Controls, Scoring, and Feedback

14.1.1 Enhancing User Controls for a Dynamic AR Game Experience

- **User-Controlled Aiming**: In an AR shooting game, user-controlled aiming can be achieved through the camera's perspective, simulating a first-person shooter experience. Add a crosshair overlay or reticle to show where shots will hit, helping users aim with precision.

- **Adding Fire and Reload Controls**: Use tap gestures to shoot and a button overlay for reloading. This ensures users have intuitive and straightforward control over the game mechanics.

yes

  o *Example Code for Fire Control*:

swift

```swift
let tapGesture = UITapGestureRecognizer(target: self,
action: #selector(fireWeapon))

sceneView.addGestureRecognizer(tapGesture)


@objc func fireWeapon(_ sender:
UITapGestureRecognizer) {
    if ammoCount > 0 {
        ammoCount -= 1
        // Trigger shooting mechanics here
    } else {
        // Show "Reload" prompt
    }
}
```

14.1.2 Scoring System and Game Progression

- **Implementing a Scoring System**: Keep track
  of the score by adding points each time a target
  is hit. Show the score on-screen to keep players
  informed of their progress. For added difficulty,
  points can vary based on the target's distance or
  difficulty level.

- **Level Progression Based on Score**: Use the score to determine when players progress to the next level. For example, advancing to a new level after reaching a score threshold or hitting a certain number of targets.

  o *Example Code for Scoring*:

swift

```swift
var score = 0

func updateScore() {
    score += 10
    scoreLabel.text = "Score: \(score)"
}
```

14.1.3 Providing Visual and Audio Feedback

- **Adding Visual Effects**: When a target is hit, apply a brief animation to signal success. Use color changes, scale transformations, or particle effects to give instant visual feedback.

- **Using Sound Effects**: Sound feedback is essential for creating an immersive experience. Add sound effects for shots fired, targets hit, and reloading to make the gameplay feel more dynamic.

- **Example Code for Visual Feedback**:

swift

```
func hitTarget(_ targetNode: SCNNode) {
    let scaleUp = SCNAction.scale(to: 1.2, duration: 0.1)
    let scaleDown = SCNAction.scale(to: 0, duration: 0.2)
    let sequence = SCNAction.sequence([scaleUp, scaleDown])
    targetNode.runAction(sequence)
    updateScore()
}
```

14.1.4 Displaying Real-Time Stats and Game Feedback

- **On-Screen Stats**: Include a HUD (Heads-Up Display) showing real-time information like score, ammo, and level progress. Position this UI at the screen edges to avoid obstructing the AR view.

- **Game Alerts and Prompts**: Use prompts or notifications to inform players of significant events, such as low ammo, time limits, or when they achieve a high score.

14.2 Integrating Physics for Gameplay Mechanics

14.2.1 Why Use Physics in AR Games?

- **Realistic Interactions**: Physics make virtual objects react naturally to user actions. In a shooting game, physics adds realism by simulating the effects of shots on targets, such as causing them to spin, fall, or bounce.

- **Enhanced Immersion**: Physics-driven interactions make virtual elements feel tangible, creating a more engaging AR experience. For example, targets that fall over when hit appear more realistic and satisfying.

14.2.2 Adding Physics to Game Objects

- **Applying Physics to Targets**: Assign SCNPhysicsBody to targets so they react to shots with physical motion, such as falling or bouncing. Dynamic physics bodies enable gravity and collisions, making targets behave realistically.

    - *Example Code for Dynamic Physics on Targets*:

swift

```
let targetGeometry = SCNSphere(radius: 0.1)
```

```swift
let targetNode = SCNNode(geometry: targetGeometry)

targetNode.physicsBody = SCNPhysicsBody(type:
.dynamic, shape: nil)

targetNode.physicsBody?.isAffectedByGravity = true

targetNode.position = SCNVector3(0, 0.5, -1)

sceneView.scene.rootNode.addChildNode(targetNode)
```

14.2.3 Using Physics for Projectiles and Collisions

- **Creating Projectiles**: Define projectiles that react to physics when fired. Projectiles should have a rigid body physics type, allowing them to move, collide with objects, and follow a defined trajectory.

- **Detecting Collisions with Targets**: Use collision detection to track when a projectile hits a target. Set up categoryBitMask and contactTestBitMask to specify which objects should trigger contact events, allowing for immediate feedback on successful hits.

  - *Example Code for Projectile Physics and Collision Detection*:

swift

```swift
let projectileGeometry = SCNSphere(radius: 0.02)

let projectileNode = SCNNode(geometry:
projectileGeometry)
```

```
projectileNode.physicsBody = SCNPhysicsBody(type:
.dynamic, shape: nil)

projectileNode.physicsBody?.velocity =
SCNVector3(0, 0, -2) // Speed of projectile

projectileNode.physicsBody?.categoryBitMask = 1 //
Projectile category

projectileNode.physicsBody?.contactTestBitMask = 2
// Target category

sceneView.scene.rootNode.addChildNode(projectileN
ode)
```

14.2.4 Reacting to Physics Events in Gameplay

- **Handling Contact Events**: Implement the physicsWorld(_:didBegin:) method to detect when the projectile hits a target. Use this method to trigger visual effects, sound feedback, and score updates when a collision occurs.

- **Example Code for Handling Contact Events**:

swift

```
func physicsWorld(_ world: SCNPhysicsWorld,
didBegin contact: SCNPhysicsContact) {

    let contactNodeA = contact.nodeA

    let contactNodeB = contact.nodeB
```

```
if contactNodeA.physicsBody?.categoryBitMask ==
1 && contactNodeB.physicsBody?.categoryBitMask
== 2 {

    // Projectile hit target

    hitTarget(contactNodeB)

  }

}
```

14.3 Testing and Refining for a Smooth Player Experience

14.3.1 Testing AR Performance and Responsiveness

- **Ensuring Smooth Frame Rates**: AR games are resource-intensive, so it's essential to test for consistent frame rates. Use lightweight assets and avoid excessive physics calculations to maintain smooth performance.

- **Testing on Multiple Devices**: Test the game on various AR-compatible devices to account for performance differences, adjusting settings like shadow quality and particle effects based on device capabilities.

14.3.2 Refining Gameplay Mechanics

- **Adjusting Game Difficulty**: Balance the difficulty by modifying factors such as target speed, size, and distance. Ensure that the game remains challenging but fair, with difficulty increasing gradually as players progress through levels.

- **Tuning Physics Properties**: Fine-tune the physics properties of objects to achieve realistic motion. For example, adjust the friction, restitution (bounciness), and damping of targets to control how they react to shots.

14.3.3 Debugging AR Game Elements

- **Debugging Visual Placement**: Use debug options, such as showing the bounding boxes of targets, to ensure they appear in the intended positions and scale.

- **Troubleshooting Physics Issues**: Adjust collision bitmasks if certain objects fail to interact as expected, or if projectiles pass through targets without triggering a hit. Ensure all interactive objects have correct collision properties.

14.3.4 Collecting and Implementing User Feedback

- **Testing with Real Users**: Conduct playtesting with users to gather feedback on controls, difficulty, and overall enjoyment. Real users can offer insights into areas for improvement that might not be apparent in development.

- **Refining Based on Feedback**: Make iterative improvements based on user feedback, adjusting elements like control responsiveness, target behavior, and scoring balance. Regular updates based on player feedback help improve engagement and retention.

14.3.5 Adding Final Touches for a Polished Experience

- **Polishing Visual and Audio Effects**: Add finishing touches to graphics and sounds to enhance the player experience. Ensure that visual effects like explosions, light flashes, and score animations align with the game's theme.

- **Creating a Start Screen and Game Over Screen**: Add UI screens for starting the game, pausing, and displaying the final score. This makes the game feel complete and gives users clear entry and exit points.

  - *Example Code for Game Over Screen*:

swift

```swift
func showGameOverScreen() {
```

```
let gameOverLabel = UILabel()

gameOverLabel.text = "Game Over"

gameOverLabel.textAlignment = .center

gameOverLabel.font =
UIFont.boldSystemFont(ofSize: 24)

gameOverLabel.frame = CGRect(x: 0, y: 0, width:
view.frame.width, height: 50)

gameOverLabel.center = view.center

view.addSubview(gameOverLabel)
}
```

14.3.6 Performance Optimization and Final Testing

- **Optimizing for Performance**: Implement techniques like object pooling to manage game assets and reduce memory usage. For example, instead of creating a new projectile each time the player fires, reuse existing projectiles.

- **Final Testing and Quality Assurance**: Perform thorough final testing to catch any last-minute bugs, ensure stability, and confirm that the game works as intended across different environments and lighting conditions. Validate that AR elements appear naturally and that the game adapts to various physical spaces.

Chapter 15: ARKit and SwiftUI for Enhanced User Experiences

15.1 Using SwiftUI for AR User Interfaces

15.1.1 Why Use SwiftUI for AR Interfaces?

- **SwiftUI Benefits**: SwiftUI is a declarative framework, making it easy to design, preview, and iterate on UIs with minimal code. When combined with ARKit, SwiftUI provides a flexible and modern approach to AR interface design, allowing developers to create clean, interactive, and dynamic layouts that enhance user experiences.

- **Integrating SwiftUI with ARKit**: Although ARKit primarily relies on UIKit, you can embed ARKit views within SwiftUI using UIViewRepresentable. This lets developers bring the power of ARKit into SwiftUI applications, combining advanced AR features with responsive and customizable SwiftUI components.

15.1.2 Setting Up ARKit in a SwiftUI Project

- **Creating the UIViewRepresentable for ARSCNView**: UIViewRepresentable is a protocol in SwiftUI that allows developers to wrap UIKit views, like ARSCNView, and use them in SwiftUI projects. Start by creating a SwiftUIARView struct that conforms to UIViewRepresentable and initializes ARSCNView with basic configuration.

- **Configuring AR Session in SwiftUI**: Initialize an AR session with ARWorldTrackingConfiguration to enable AR functionality. In this example, we'll enable horizontal plane detection for placing objects in the real-world environment.

  o *Example Code for UIViewRepresentable*:

swift

```swift
import SwiftUI
import ARKit

struct SwiftUIARView: UIViewRepresentable {
    func makeUIView(context: Context) -> ARSCNView {
        let arView = ARSCNView(frame: .zero)
```

```swift
        let configuration =
ARWorldTrackingConfiguration()

        configuration.planeDetection = [.horizontal]

        arView.session.run(configuration)

        return arView

    }


    func updateUIView(_ uiView: ARSCNView,
context: Context) {}

}
```

15.1.3 Customizing AR Elements with SwiftUI Controls

- **Adding UI Controls Over ARSCNView**: Use SwiftUI components like buttons, sliders, and text overlays to control AR interactions. By layering these SwiftUI views over ARSCNView, you can create controls for actions such as object placement, navigation, and toggling AR elements.

- **Example Code for Adding SwiftUI Buttons**:

swift

```swift
struct ContentView: View {
  var body: some View {
```

```swift
ZStack {
    SwiftUIARView() // Embeds AR view
    VStack {
        Button(action: {
            // Action for placing object in AR
        }) {
            Text("Place Object")
                .padding()
                .background(Color.blue)
                .foregroundColor(.white)
                .cornerRadius(8)
        }
        .padding()
    }
}
}
```

15.2 Creating AR Interfaces That Are Responsive and User-Friendly

15.2.1 Designing a User-Friendly AR Interface with SwiftUI

- **Minimizing Interface Clutter**: AR experiences are immersive, so UI elements should be minimal and unobtrusive. Use simple buttons and labels for essential controls only, and ensure they do not obscure the AR content.

- **Using SwiftUI's State-Driven Approach**: SwiftUI's declarative syntax and state-driven updates allow for smoother, more responsive interactions. By using @State and @Binding properties, you can easily track and update interface elements based on user actions or AR events.

  - *Example Code for Responsive Controls*:

swift

```
struct ContentView: View {
```

```swift
@State private var objectPlaced = false


var body: some View {
  ZStack {
    SwiftUIARView()
    VStack {
      Button(action: {
        objectPlaced.toggle()
      }) {
        Text(objectPlaced ? "Remove Object" : "Place Object")
          .padding()
          .background(objectPlaced ? Color.red : Color.blue)
          .foregroundColor(.white)
          .cornerRadius(8)
      }
      .padding()
    }
  }
}
```

```
}
```

15.2.2 Enhancing Interactivity with SwiftUI Animations

- **SwiftUI Animation Capabilities**: SwiftUI's built-in animations make it easy to add transitions, fades, and other effects to UI elements. For example, a "Place Object" button could smoothly fade out after being pressed, creating a cleaner user experience.

- **Applying Animation to AR Controls**: Use SwiftUI's .animation modifier to apply smooth transitions between UI states. This enhances the experience by providing feedback for actions, making the interface feel dynamic and intuitive.

  - *Example Code for Animated Controls*:

swift

```swift
struct ContentView: View {

    @State private var showButton = true

    var body: some View {
        ZStack {
            SwiftUIARView()
            if showButton {
```

```
Button("Place Object") {

    showButton = false

}
.padding()
.background(Color.blue)
.foregroundColor(.white)
.cornerRadius(8)
.transition(.opacity)
.animation(.easeInOut(duration: 0.5))

    }

}

}

}
```

15.2.3 Accessibility and Usability in AR Interfaces

- **Ensuring Accessibility**: AR applications should consider accessibility, ensuring controls are large and easily reachable on the screen. Use colors with adequate contrast and implement VoiceOver compatibility for visually impaired users.

- **Using Dynamic Type for Text**: SwiftUI supports dynamic type, which adjusts font sizes based on user settings. Integrating this feature into the AR app ensures readability across various accessibility preferences.

15.3 Example Project: Building an AR Gallery with SwiftUI

15.3.1 Project Overview

- **Objective**: Build an AR gallery where users can view and interact with virtual artwork or images in an AR environment. Users can place art pieces on detected surfaces and navigate through the gallery using SwiftUI controls.

- **Features**:

  o Place and remove artwork in the AR environment.

  o Swipe to navigate through a gallery of images.

  o Provide basic information about each art piece.

15.3.2 Setting Up the AR Gallery Scene

- **Initializing the AR View**: Use UIViewRepresentable to create the ARSCNView and run ARWorldTrackingConfiguration with plane detection enabled. This will allow the placement of artwork on real-world surfaces.

- **Example Code for AR Setup**:

swift

```swift
struct SwiftUIARView: UIViewRepresentable {
    func makeUIView(context: Context) -> ARSCNView {
        let arView = ARSCNView(frame: .zero)
        let configuration = ARWorldTrackingConfiguration()
        configuration.planeDetection = [.horizontal]
        arView.session.run(configuration)
        return arView
    }

    func updateUIView(_ uiView: ARSCNView, context: Context) {}
}
```

15.3.3 Creating the Gallery with SwiftUI

- **Gallery Data and State**: Define a list of images and titles representing the artwork. Use @State to track the current artwork index and update it when users swipe to view different pieces.

- **Example Code for Gallery Data**:

swift

```
struct Artwork {
    let image: String
    let title: String
}


struct ContentView: View {
    @State private var artworkIndex = 0
    let gallery = [
        Artwork(image: "art1", title: "Mona Lisa"),
        Artwork(image: "art2", title: "Starry Night"),
        Artwork(image: "art3", title: "The Scream")
    ]
}
```

15.3.4 Placing Artwork in AR

- **Adding Artwork Nodes**: When users tap "Place Artwork," the app will add a node with the selected artwork image to the AR scene.

Using SCNPlane, create a 3D representation of the artwork and add it to ARSCNView.

- **Example Code for Placing Artwork**:

swift

```swift
struct SwiftUIARView: UIViewRepresentable {
    let artwork: Artwork

    func makeUIView(context: Context) -> ARSCNView {
        let arView = ARSCNView(frame: .zero)
        let configuration = ARWorldTrackingConfiguration()
        configuration.planeDetection = [.horizontal]
        arView.session.run(configuration)
        return arView
    }

    func updateUIView(_ uiView: ARSCNView, context: Context) {
        // Clear previous artwork
```

```
uiView.scene.rootNode.childNodes.forEach {
$0.removeFromParentNode() }
```

```
// Create new artwork node

let plane = SCNPlane(width: 0.3, height: 0.4)

plane.firstMaterial?.diffuse.contents =
UIImage(named: artwork.image)

let artworkNode = SCNNode(geometry: plane)

artworkNode.position = SCNVector3(0, 0, -1) //
Place 1 meter in front
```

```
uiView.scene.rootNode.addChildNode(artworkNode)

    }

}
```

15.3.5 Navigating the Gallery with Swipe Gestures

- **Adding Swipe Controls**: Use SwiftUI's gesture system to navigate the gallery. A left swipe increments the artwork index, while a right swipe decrements it, allowing users to view different pieces.

- **Example Code for Swipe Gestures**:

swift

```swift
struct ContentView: View {
    @State private var artworkIndex = 0
    let gallery = [
        Artwork(image: "art1", title: "Mona Lisa"),
        Artwork(image: "art2", title: "Starry Night"),
        Artwork(image: "art3", title: "The Scream")
    ]

    var body: some View {
        ZStack {
            SwiftUIARView(artwork: gallery[artworkIndex])
            VStack {
                Text(gallery[artworkIndex].title)
                    .font(.headline)
                    .padding()

                HStack {
                    Button(action: { previousArtwork() }) {
                        Image(systemName: "arrow.left")
                            .padding()
```

```
            }

        Button(action: { nextArtwork() }) {
            Image(systemName: "arrow.right")
                .padding()
            }
          }
        }
      }
    .gesture(DragGesture().onEnded { value in
        if value.translation.width < 0 { nextArtwork() }
        else { previousArtwork() }
      })
    }


func nextArtwork() {
    artworkIndex = (artworkIndex + 1) %
gallery.count
    }


func previousArtwork() {
```

```
    artworkIndex = (artworkIndex - 1 + gallery.count)
% gallery.count

    }

}
```

15.3.6 Enhancing the AR Gallery with Additional Features

- **Adding Artwork Information Overlays**: Display information about each art piece, like the artist or historical context, as an overlay. This can enhance the gallery experience, making it educational as well as interactive.

- **Applying Animations**: Use SwiftUI animations to make transitions between artworks smooth and visually appealing. For instance, apply a fade transition when artwork changes to make it look seamless.

15.3.7 Testing and Finalizing the AR Gallery

- **Testing Responsiveness and Usability**: Run the AR gallery on different devices to test its responsiveness. Check that UI elements respond quickly and accurately and that the artwork placement remains stable within the AR environment.

- **Fine-Tuning UI Elements**: Adjust the size, position, and opacity of UI elements to ensure they are easy to see and use without obstructing the view of the AR content.

Chapter 16: Optimizing AR Performance for iOS

16.1 Techniques for Efficient AR App Performance

16.1.1 Why Performance Optimization Matters in AR

- **AR Performance Challenges**: Augmented Reality (AR) applications require significant resources to blend virtual and real-world elements seamlessly. High-quality AR performance involves rendering complex 3D objects, processing camera data, and tracking spatial orientation in real time. These tasks can strain an iOS device's CPU, GPU, and battery.

- **User Experience and Engagement**: For an immersive AR experience, performance is essential. Lagging, freezing, or jerky animations break the immersive experience, leading to frustration and diminished user engagement. By optimizing performance, you ensure a smooth, enjoyable experience that keeps users engaged.

16.1.2 Techniques for Efficient Rendering in ARKit

- **Optimize Object Rendering**: In AR, rendering lightweight 3D models is essential for performance. Use simplified models with low polygon counts, especially for background objects, to minimize rendering time.

- **Use Efficient Textures and Materials**: Instead of using high-resolution textures, optimize image file sizes by compressing them. Consider using basic materials and avoid complex shaders, which can slow down rendering. Leverage texture atlases, where multiple textures are combined into one, reducing draw calls and improving efficiency.

- **Implement Level of Detail (LOD)**: Adjust the level of detail on objects based on their distance from the user. For example, objects that are further away don't need as much detail as those close to the camera. Use low-polygon versions of objects for distant elements and switch to higher-polygon versions as objects come closer.

  o *Example Code for Switching LOD*:

swift

```
let farObject = SCNNode(geometry:
SCNSphere(radius: 0.1))
```

```
let nearObject = SCNNode(geometry:
SCNSphere(radius: 0.3))

if distanceToCamera < 1.0 {

    farObject.removeFromParentNode()


sceneView.scene.rootNode.addChildNode(nearObject)

} else {

    nearObject.removeFromParentNode()


sceneView.scene.rootNode.addChildNode(farObject)

}
```

16.1.3 Optimizing Lighting and Shadows

- **Use Realistic, But Simple Lighting**: Although realistic lighting enhances the AR experience, too many light sources or complex lighting effects can hinder performance. Try to use a single directional light for basic illumination and ambient light for softening. Avoid using multiple light sources unless absolutely necessary.

- **Reduce Shadow Complexity**: Shadows improve depth perception but can be resource-intensive. If shadows are essential, consider using soft shadows or reducing the shadow resolution to balance realism with performance.

Avoid enabling shadows on all objects; apply them selectively to high-impact elements only.

16.1.4 Minimizing Physics Calculations

- **Simplify Physics Interactions**: Use physics sparingly and only for key objects that need interactions. Setting objects to static rather than dynamic can improve performance as static objects don't require continuous physics calculations.

- **Use Simplified Physics Shapes**: Instead of complex geometry for collision detection, use basic shapes like boxes, spheres, or capsules. Simplified shapes reduce the workload on the physics engine, allowing it to handle interactions more efficiently.

  - *Example Code for Simplified Physics Body*:

swift

```swift
let simpleBox = SCNBox(width: 1.0, height: 1.0, length: 1.0, chamferRadius: 0)

let physicsBody = SCNPhysicsBody(type: .static, shape: SCNPhysicsShape(geometry: simpleBox, options: nil))

let objectNode = SCNNode(geometry: simpleBox)

objectNode.physicsBody = physicsBody
```

```
sceneView.scene.rootNode.addChildNode(objectNode
)
```

16.2 Managing Memory, Frame Rates, and Battery Life in AR Apps

16.2.1 Memory Management for AR Apps

- **Limit 3D Object and Texture Loading**: Large textures and high-polygon models consume more memory. Consider dynamically loading and unloading textures or models based on proximity to the user. Load only what's necessary for the immediate environment.

- **Use Asset Compression and Caching**: Compress assets where possible to reduce memory usage. For models, use formats like USDZ or compressed .scn files. Caching frequently used assets also saves time and reduces memory load.

- **Monitor and Release Resources**: Track memory usage and release resources when they're no longer needed. Implement willDisappear events to clear unused assets and avoid memory leaks.

16.2.2 Achieving Smooth Frame Rates

- **Targeting 60 FPS or Higher**: A smooth AR experience requires a frame rate of 60 frames per second (FPS) or higher. Regularly monitor frame rates and identify areas where performance drops, optimizing any identified bottlenecks.

- **Batch Processing and Reducing Draw Calls**: Minimize the number of separate draw calls by grouping objects or reducing the number of distinct shaders and textures. Each additional draw call can slow performance, especially in a complex scene.

- **Optimize Animations**: Limit the use of animations that involve intensive transformations (e.g., rotation or scaling). Instead of continuously running animations, consider using triggered animations that occur only when the user interacts with the object.

16.2.3 Battery Life Considerations

- **Optimize Background Processes**: Background tasks, such as continuous plane detection, can consume significant battery life. Pause background processes when they aren't needed, such as pausing plane detection after the initial setup.

- **Adjust AR Session Quality**: Lowering the quality of the AR session (e.g., reducing the frame rate slightly or using lower-resolution textures) can extend battery life, especially on older devices.

- **Implement Energy-Saving Modes**: Give users the option to enable a low-power mode, which could turn off non-essential features like shadows, physics, or complex animations to save battery life.

16.3 Practical Tips: Optimization Strategies for Smooth AR Experiences

16.3.1 Using Metal for Enhanced Performance

- **What is Metal?** Metal is Apple's graphics and compute API, optimized for high-performance graphics rendering. Using Metal with ARKit allows for more control over rendering, reducing CPU and GPU load for complex scenes.

- **Creating a Metal Layer in ARKit**: You can combine Metal with ARSCNView to render objects with high efficiency, especially useful for complex scenes that require optimized graphics processing.

- *Example Code for Metal Integration*:

swift

```
let device = MTLCreateSystemDefaultDevice()
let metalLayer = CAMetalLayer()
```

```swift
metalLayer.device = device

metalLayer.pixelFormat = .bgra8Unorm

metalLayer.framebufferOnly = true

metalLayer.contentsScale = UIScreen.main.scale

sceneView.layer.addSublayer(metalLayer)
```

16.3.2 Efficient Use of ARKit's Plane Detection

- **Selective Plane Detection**: Enable plane detection only for specific surfaces (horizontal or vertical) to reduce computational load. For example, if your app requires only horizontal surfaces, disable vertical plane detection.

- **Dynamic Plane Detection Control**: Start with plane detection enabled, but once surfaces are identified, disable plane detection to save resources. Re-enable it only if users need to reconfigure the environment.

  - *Example Code for Disabling Plane Detection*:

swift

```swift
let configuration = ARWorldTrackingConfiguration()

configuration.planeDetection = []

sceneView.session.run(configuration, options:
[.resetTracking, .removeExistingAnchors])
```

16.3.3 Managing Audio and Haptics for Optimal Performance

- **Optimize Audio Effects**: Use lightweight audio formats (e.g., AAC or MP3) and avoid looping audio unnecessarily, as it can increase CPU usage and affect battery life. Load sounds only when needed and release them after use.

- **Using Haptic Feedback Sparingly**: While haptic feedback enhances user experience, excessive or continuous haptic events can strain the battery. Use it strategically for high-impact moments, such as a successful interaction or a level completion.

16.3.4 Reducing Memory and Performance Load with Object Pooling

- **What is Object Pooling?** Object pooling involves reusing instances of objects, particularly in scenarios like projectiles, where creating and deleting objects repeatedly can drain resources. Pool objects and reuse them as needed to save memory and processing power.

- **Implementing Object Pooling for Projectiles**:
  - Initialize a pool of projectiles when the app launches and retrieve unused projectiles from the pool as needed.
  - *Example Code for Object Pooling*:

swift

```swift
var projectilePool: [SCNNode] = []

func createProjectile() -> SCNNode {
    if let projectile = projectilePool.first {
        projectilePool.removeFirst()
        return projectile
    } else {
        let newProjectile = SCNNode(geometry: SCNSphere(radius: 0.05))
        newProjectile.physicsBody = SCNPhysicsBody(type: .dynamic, shape: nil)
        return newProjectile
    }
}

func returnToPool(projectile: SCNNode) {
    projectilePool.append(projectile)
    projectile.removeFromParentNode()
}
```

16.3.5 Testing and Debugging for Optimization

- **Use Xcode Instruments**: Xcode's Instruments tool provides deep insights into resource usage. Tools like Time Profiler, Allocations, and Energy Log help identify memory leaks, CPU bottlenecks, and battery-intensive operations, offering a data-driven approach to optimization.

- **Profile on Multiple Devices**: Test the AR experience on various iOS devices, especially older ones, to ensure smooth performance across different hardware capabilities. This helps identify device-specific issues and optimize accordingly.

- **Optimize for Real-World Conditions**: Test the app in different lighting conditions, environments, and distances. AR performance can vary based on environmental factors, and real-world testing helps ensure the app works consistently under varied conditions.

16.3.6 Balancing Quality and Performance

- **Compromise Strategically**: Find the balance between visual quality and performance. While high-quality textures, lighting, and animations improve the AR experience, they also demand more processing power. Assess which features are most critical for the user experience and optimize others to meet performance goals.

- **Implement User Options**: Allow users to adjust performance settings, such as a "Quality

Mode" for high-end devices and a "Performance Mode" for older devices. This gives users control over their experience and ensures smooth gameplay across different device models.

Chapter 17: Publishing and Marketing Your AR App

17.1 Preparing Your AR App for the App Store: Guidelines and Tips

17.1.1 Meeting Apple's App Store Guidelines for AR Apps

- **Compliance with App Store Review Guidelines**: Ensure your app aligns with Apple's general guidelines, including functionality, design, and privacy requirements. For AR apps, it's especially important to address user safety and battery optimization due to their resource-intensive nature.

- **Focusing on Safety and Usability**: Apple is particularly cautious about AR apps that encourage user mobility. Include prompts or warnings reminding users to be aware of their surroundings. Design the app to avoid features that may cause disorientation or encourage unsafe behaviors.

- **Ensuring Accessibility**: Incorporate accessibility features, like VoiceOver support for screen readers, larger touch targets, and text contrast adjustments. Accessible AR apps reach a wider audience, and Apple often highlights accessible apps.

17.1.2 Optimizing App Performance and Battery Usage

- **Testing for Performance Stability**: AR apps can consume significant resources. Run your app through performance tests on multiple iOS devices to ensure a smooth, stable experience. Test under various lighting and environmental conditions, as AR tracking can vary.

- **Reducing Battery Consumption**: Apple discourages apps that drain battery excessively. Techniques like optimizing asset loading, disabling unnecessary background tasks, and offering a low-power mode can enhance battery efficiency, making the app more appealing to Apple reviewers and users alike.

- **Preparing for Different Device Capabilities**: Ensure the app runs well on older devices as well as newer ones. Use conditional code for device-specific features or offer an "Optimized for Newer Devices" option so that users with high-performance devices can access advanced settings.

17.1.3 Setting Up a Compelling App Store Page

- **Creating High-Quality Screenshots and Videos**: Use the first few images and video frames to showcase the app's core AR features. Highlight the AR experience and include clear shots of what users will see and interact with in the app. Consider using a screen recording on a blank wall or table for a clean, distraction-free view.

- **Writing an Engaging App Description**: Describe the core features and functionality of your AR app in a clear, engaging way. Emphasize what sets your app apart, whether it's a unique user experience, groundbreaking AR features, or something else compelling.

- **Adding Relevant Keywords**: Keywords impact search visibility. Include terms like "AR," "Augmented Reality," "3D," and other relevant descriptors, ensuring they reflect how users would search for your app.

17.2 App Store Optimization (ASO) Strategies for AR Apps

17.2.1 Understanding App Store Optimization (ASO)

- **What is ASO?** ASO is the process of optimizing your app's visibility and ranking in app store search results. Effective ASO boosts your app's exposure, making it more discoverable to potential users. For AR apps, ASO includes targeting keywords related to augmented reality, interaction, and immersive experiences.

- **Importance of ASO for AR Apps**: AR is still an emerging technology, and users often search for AR-specific features. Effective ASO helps attract users interested in innovative experiences and can differentiate your app from others that may not emphasize AR.

17.2.2 Choosing Effective Keywords

- **Researching Relevant Keywords**: Use tools like App Annie, Sensor Tower, or Apple's own App Analytics to research popular keywords within the AR category. Include terms like "Augmented Reality," "AR game," "3D interactions," and "real-world overlay."

- **Targeting Long-Tail Keywords**: Long-tail keywords are phrases rather than single words and are more specific (e.g., "AR interior design app" or "3D interactive learning"). Although long-tail keywords have lower search volume, they attract more relevant users, increasing the likelihood of app downloads.

- **Updating Keywords Regularly**: Track your app's performance and adjust keywords based on trends and analytics. AR is a rapidly evolving space, so updating keywords ensures your app remains aligned with current search trends.

17.2.3 Optimizing App Name and Subtitle

- **Crafting an Engaging App Name**: The app name should be memorable, reflect its core functionality, and, if possible, include a primary keyword. For example, if your app is a virtual gallery, a name like "ArtView AR: Virtual Art Gallery" provides both branding and discoverability.

- **Writing an Effective Subtitle**: The subtitle appears below the app name and offers an additional opportunity for keyword optimization. Describe what makes your app unique in a few words, using AR-related terms where possible. For instance, "Explore 3D Art with Augmented Reality."

17.2.4 Creating an Eye-Catching App Icon

- **Designing an Icon that Reflects AR**: Use a simple, bold design that conveys the app's purpose. An effective AR app icon can incorporate elements like 3D shapes, spatial cues, or vibrant colors, suggesting the app's immersive, interactive nature.

- **A/B Testing Icon Variations**: Test several icon designs to find the one that resonates best with users. Some design variations may perform better than others, even with minor changes. Use tools like SplitMetrics or StoreMaven for A/B testing.

17.3 Promoting Your AR App: Marketing Channels and Best Practices

17.3.1 Leveraging Social Media Marketing

- **Building Awareness on Visual Platforms**: Social media platforms like Instagram, TikTok, and YouTube are ideal for AR app marketing, as they support visual storytelling. Share videos demonstrating your app's unique AR features and highlight interactive elements.

- **Engaging with the AR Community**: Connect with AR enthusiasts, developers, and influencers on platforms like Twitter, LinkedIn, and Reddit. Engaging with online communities dedicated to AR and VR can expand your reach, as these audiences are often eager to explore new AR experiences.

- **Using Paid Advertising for Targeted Reach**: Use paid ads on Facebook, Instagram, and TikTok to reach a targeted audience. Social media platforms offer precise targeting, enabling you to advertise to users based on interests in AR, VR, technology, and mobile gaming.

17.3.2 Creating a Compelling Demo Video

- **Showcasing Core Features in the Video**: A demo video should capture the app's core AR features within the first few seconds. Show a user interacting with AR objects and highlight what makes your app unique, whether it's the user interface, interactivity, or visual effects.

- **Keeping the Video Concise and Engaging**: Aim for a video length of 15 to 30 seconds. Cover essential aspects like navigation, interactivity, and ease of use without overwhelming the viewer. Use engaging visuals and a dynamic pace to retain attention.

- **Publishing on YouTube and App Preview**: Upload the demo video on YouTube, which has a large reach and is SEO-friendly. Embed the video on your website and share it across other social media platforms. Apple also allows preview videos on the App Store, where you can highlight the AR experience directly on your app page.

17.3.3 Influencer Marketing and Partnerships

- **Collaborating with AR Enthusiasts and Influencers**: Partner with influencers who specialize in tech, AR, or VR. Influencers can create sponsored content showcasing your app, and their followers are likely to be interested in new AR experiences.

- **Seeking Partnerships with Complementary Apps or Products**: Partner with apps or brands that align with your AR app's focus. For instance, if you're promoting an AR interior design app, collaborating with home decor brands or design influencers can increase exposure.

- **Using User-Generated Content (UGC)**: Encourage users to share their experiences with your AR app on social media by incentivizing them with challenges or rewards. UGC builds credibility and acts as organic marketing, allowing potential users to see others interacting with the app.

17.3.4 Engaging Users through Content Marketing

- **Writing Blog Posts and Tutorials**: Publish blog posts on your website about the features, updates, and use cases of your AR app. Tutorials and how-to articles can also attract users interested in learning about AR.

- **Building an Email List for Updates**: Encourage users to sign up for updates, especially if you plan to release new features or content. Email marketing helps retain existing users by providing value, such as usage tips or exclusive content.

- **Publishing Guest Posts on AR and Tech Websites**: Reach out to AR, tech, or mobile app-focused websites to publish guest articles or have your app featured. A review or article on a well-regarded tech site adds credibility and attracts potential users.

17.3.5 Utilizing App Store Promotions and Apple's Features

- **Promoting Your App with In-App Events**: Apple's in-app events feature allows you to promote time-sensitive activities directly on the App Store. For example, if your AR app has seasonal events or special content releases, you can feature these as in-app events to attract attention.

- **Applying for Apple's "Featured App" Section**: Apple frequently showcases innovative AR apps. By aligning with Apple's goals—such as offering a unique user experience, accessibility, or technology innovation—your app has a chance to be featured, which greatly boosts downloads and visibility.

- **Offering Limited-Time Promotions**: Temporary discounts or premium feature trials can drive new users to try your app. Promoted offers, like in-app purchases or subscriptions, can be highlighted on your App Store page, attracting users who appreciate time-limited incentives.

17.3.6 Leveraging Analytics and Iterative Improvements

- **Monitoring Performance with Analytics Tools**: Track user behavior and engagement metrics using tools like App Analytics, Google Firebase, or Mixpanel. These insights help you understand how users interact with your app and identify areas for improvement.

- **Gathering and Analyzing User Feedback**: Encourage users to leave reviews on the App Store and listen to their feedback. Many users may have suggestions or point out bugs that you missed, offering invaluable insights for future updates.

- **Updating Regularly Based on Data**: Use the analytics data and user feedback to guide improvements in performance, functionality, and design. Regular updates show that the app is actively maintained, improving its credibility and user trust.

Chapter 18: Future of AR and Continuous Learning

18.1 Emerging Trends in AR and Potential New Features in ARKit

18.1.1 Current Trends Driving AR Forward

- **Increased Adoption of AR Across Industries**: AR has gained traction in fields like retail, education, healthcare, and real estate. Retailers use AR to let customers try products virtually, while educators create immersive learning experiences. Healthcare providers use AR for training, and real estate agents offer AR tours of properties. This broad adoption highlights AR's versatility and its growing impact on daily life.

- **Expansion of AR in Social Media and Entertainment**: Social platforms like Instagram, Snapchat, and TikTok incorporate AR filters and effects, showing how users embrace interactive AR experiences. This trend emphasizes the role of AR in content creation and social engagement, making it easier for everyday users to experiment with AR.

18.1.2 Key Technologies Shaping the Future of AR

- **5G Connectivity for Real-Time AR Experiences**: The deployment of 5G networks is set to improve AR's real-time responsiveness, allowing high-speed data transfer with minimal latency. This is crucial for applications that require rapid interactions and feedback, such as multiplayer AR games, collaborative AR, and real-time navigation.

- **AI Integration for Enhanced Recognition and Interaction**: Combining AI with AR will advance object and gesture recognition, leading to more personalized and context-aware experiences. AI-powered AR can enable virtual assistants to provide information based on recognized objects, making AR experiences more intelligent and adaptive.

- **Advances in Hardware: AR Glasses and Wearables**: The development of wearable AR devices, such as AR glasses, allows for hands-free, continuous experiences. Companies like Apple, Google, and Microsoft are investing in AR hardware, hinting at future mainstream adoption of wearable AR, where users interact with AR applications seamlessly throughout the day.

18.1.3 Potential New Features in ARKit

- **Body Tracking and Full-Body Motion Capture**: ARKit currently supports face and hand tracking, but the future may bring full-body tracking capabilities. This could allow for applications like fitness coaching, where AR monitors the user's posture, or interactive gaming, where a player's entire body movements control virtual avatars.

- **Object Permanence and Environment Persistence**: Currently, AR experiences reset when the app is closed, but object permanence would allow AR elements to remain in place even after the app restarts. Persistent AR enables users to create virtual notes or decorations in their homes that stay visible every time they open the app.

- **Improved Occlusion Capabilities**: Occlusion, or the ability of AR objects to be hidden by real-world objects, is limited in current ARKit versions. Future iterations could allow more natural interactions, where AR elements realistically disappear behind or interact with real-world objects, enhancing immersion.

18.2 Expanding Your AR Knowledge: Resources and Communities

18.2.1 Online Courses and Tutorials for AR Development

- **Apple's Official ARKit Documentation**: Apple provides comprehensive ARKit documentation covering setup, features, and best practices. The documentation is ideal for developers seeking a foundational understanding of ARKit's capabilities.

- **Online Learning Platforms (e.g., Udacity, Coursera, Udemy)**: These platforms offer courses on AR, including ARKit, Unity, and Unreal Engine. Courses on Swift development combined with ARKit tutorials provide a strong foundation for creating iOS AR applications.

- **YouTube Channels Focused on AR Development**: Channels like The AR/VR Journey and Unity's official YouTube page offer tutorials, tips, and project ideas for AR developers of all levels. Video tutorials are excellent for learning visually and understanding practical use cases in AR.

18.2.2 Engaging with AR Communities

- **Stack Overflow and AR Subreddits**: Platforms like Stack Overflow and Reddit have active communities of AR developers and enthusiasts. Participating in these forums helps developers get answers to technical questions, share projects, and discover innovative ideas.

- **LinkedIn and Meetup AR Groups**: LinkedIn groups and local Meetup events bring AR professionals and enthusiasts together to network, discuss emerging trends, and collaborate on projects. Many Meetups also host virtual events, making it easy to join from anywhere.

- **GitHub Repositories and Open-Source Projects**: Many developers share ARKit and Unity projects on GitHub. Studying these open-source projects is valuable for understanding different coding approaches, solving common AR challenges, and discovering innovative use cases. Contributing to AR repositories also allows developers to gain experience and connect with others in the community.

18.2.3 Books and Publications on AR and Related Technologies

- **"Augmented Reality: Principles and Practice" by Dieter Schmalstieg and Tobias Hollerer**: This book covers the technical aspects of AR, including the mathematics and algorithms behind it. It's an excellent resource for developers seeking a deeper understanding of AR's underlying principles.

- **"Learning Swift" by Jonathon Manning, Paris Buttfield-Addison, and Tim Nugent**: For those developing ARKit apps, learning Swift is essential. This book covers Swift basics, making it a valuable starting point for iOS developers.

- **Industry Journals and Blogs**: Publications like IEEE Computer Graphics and Applications often publish articles on AR innovations. Following tech blogs like TechCrunch and ARPost keeps developers informed on the latest advancements, partnerships, and product launches in the AR field.

18.3 Long-Term Outlook: How AR is Shaping Future User Experiences

18.3.1 AR's Impact on Everyday Life and Productivity

- **Enhanced Shopping and Retail Experiences**: AR lets users preview products virtually, enabling retailers to create immersive shopping experiences. Customers can view how furniture looks in their homes or try on clothing virtually. This trend is likely to expand, leading to more personalized and accessible retail.

- **AR in Workplace Collaboration and Remote Work**: As remote work increases, AR offers tools for immersive collaboration. Virtual meeting platforms are beginning to incorporate AR elements, allowing remote teams to share 3D models, annotate virtual objects, and work together in a virtual environment.

- **Augmented Learning and Training**: AR is transforming education, particularly in fields like medicine, engineering, and vocational training. Students can interact with complex models (like the human anatomy or machinery) through AR, gaining hands-on experience in a risk-free environment.

18.3.2 Revolutionizing Travel, Navigation, and Exploration

- **Real-Time Navigation and Mapping**: AR-enhanced navigation allows users to see directions overlayed on real-world environments, making navigation more intuitive. This is useful in crowded or unfamiliar places, where traditional maps may not suffice. Future applications could integrate real-time data, showing nearby points of interest, traffic conditions, and more.

- **Tourism and Cultural Exploration**: AR is creating immersive travel experiences. Museums, landmarks, and historic sites are using AR to overlay digital information on exhibits, offering tourists interactive and educational experiences. In the future, AR could make cultural education more accessible by bringing historical events and artifacts to life virtually.

18.3.3 How AR is Changing Healthcare and Therapy

- **AR in Surgical Training and Procedures**: Surgeons are using AR to visualize complex procedures, overlaying 3D models onto a patient's body to guide incisions or mark areas of interest. AR can also provide real-time patient data, such as heart rate and blood pressure, enhancing the precision and safety of surgical procedures.

- **AR for Physical and Mental Health Therapy**: AR offers new methods for physical therapy, allowing therapists to create interactive exercises and track patient progress in real time. In mental health, AR exposure therapy enables patients to confront phobias or anxiety triggers in a controlled, virtual environment, aiding in treatment.

18.3.4 The Future of AR in Gaming and Entertainment

- **Immersive Gaming with AR Glasses**: As AR glasses and wearables evolve, gaming is expected to shift from handheld devices to immersive experiences. AR games will move beyond the screen, with players interacting in real-world spaces where virtual elements are projected, creating fully immersive experiences.

- **Live Events and Interactive Entertainment**: AR is already being used in sports, concerts, and other live events to enhance the audience experience. Imagine watching a live sports game with AR overlays displaying real-time stats, player profiles, and interactive replays. This trend could expand to theater, concerts, and virtual events, offering audiences new ways to engage with performances.

18.3.5 Potential Challenges and Ethical Considerations for AR's Future

- **Privacy and Security Concerns**: As AR becomes more integrated into daily life, the technology will gather significant amounts of personal data, such as location, environment, and user interactions. Ensuring data privacy and protecting against security threats will be essential to maintain user trust.

- **Social and Psychological Impacts**: Prolonged AR use could have social and psychological effects, from dependence on virtual enhancements to challenges with distinguishing between virtual and real experiences. Researchers and developers will need to assess and address the potential long-term impacts of AR on mental health and social interactions.

- **Environmental and Energy Implications**: AR applications require substantial processing power and battery usage, which can strain devices and energy resources. Sustainable practices in AR development and hardware, such as efficient battery usage and recyclable

AR glasses, will be critical as the technology becomes more widespread.

18.3.6 Vision for AR's Role in Future Technologies

- **Integration with the Internet of Things (IoT)**: As IoT devices become more common, AR can serve as an interface for interacting with these connected devices. Users could control home appliances, check data from health monitors, and receive alerts through AR, making interactions with IoT devices more intuitive.

- **Blending AR with VR and the Metaverse**: The convergence of AR and VR into a unified metaverse experience could create a digital world where users move seamlessly between augmented and fully virtual environments. This blending offers endless possibilities, from attending a work meeting in VR to viewing AR-enhanced data overlays in the real world.

- **The Rise of Spatial Computing**: Spatial computing combines AI, AR, VR, and IoT to create highly interactive and intelligent environments. AR is a key component of spatial computing, enabling users to interact with data and virtual objects embedded within real-world spaces, transforming how we access and use digital information.